THE COURAGE TO CHANGE THE THINGS I CAN

In

Christ's

Awesome

Love

Mike A Hill

Accent Digital Publishing, Inc.
2932 Churn Creek Rd
Redding, CA 96002
(530) 223-0202

www.accentdigitalpublishing.com

ISBN 978-60445-057-6

You can email Mike Hill at chainsaw.mike@hotmail.com or
post a comment at www.thecouragebook.blogspot.com.
To order books, visit www.accentdigital@gmail.com
(530-223-0202)

THE COURAGE TO CHANGE THE THINGS I CAN

BY MIKE "CHAINSAW" HILL

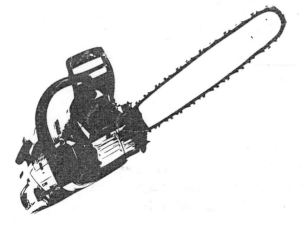

DEDICATION

This book is dedicated to God, every member of my family, and every person who has touched my life. Kathleen Robertson at Good Books, Rodney and Rebecca Boudreau, Dan and Laurie Woolery, and Avery Vilche–the toughest female MMA fighter I've ever seen–who inspired me to write this book in the first place.

A special thanks to everyone, even the readers of my story: The people of NA (Narcotics Anonymous) and my churches especially. Shaleen, my beloved wife, you have been right along side of me through the good and the bad and everywhere in between- you are my life partner. Justin and Winston Hill, my two sons, whom I will be reunited with one day soon. All of my other kids—Lacey, Kacey and Jayce— you've put up with a lot. I love you.

The entire staff at Accent Digital Publishing deserve words of praise for their hard work and belief in me. Chase Knudsen, thank you for your friendship and generous gift of time and help, as well.

I just want to add that people DO change. I'm living proof! And I know that Jesus Christ, the King of Kings, has great things in store for me and my life, as long as I'm willing to stay teachable, open minded and honest with myself and others. Thank you, God.

"The Serenity Prayer"

by Dr. Reinhold Niebuhr

God grant me the serenity to accept the things I cannot change,
Courage to change the things I can change,
And the wisdom to know the difference.

Living one day at a time;

Enjoying one moment at a time;

Accepting hardships as the pathway to peace;
Taking, as He did, this sinful world as it is, not as I would have it;

Trusting that He will make all things right if I surrender to His will;

That I may be reasonably happy in this life and supremely happy with Him forever in the next.
Amen.

Contents

CHAPTER 1
A Convict In Training

This is a story for anyone who is lost or knows someone who is lost. It's a story of hope and change. It is proof that anyone, even the worst of the worst, can overcome great obstacles and find happiness. My name is Mike Hill. I was born to two teenagers on June 7, 1966. I came into this world in a birthing home for unwed mothers in a small southern California town called Montrose. My mother couldn't keep me, and I was soon adopted by Robert and Deanna Hill. It was actually their daughter, Teri, who picked me out of around six other adoptees. We joke that I was the pick of the litter! I say this in a humorous way as that's kinda been the way the story goes; sure enough, she picked me, just like a speckled little pup.

So there we were, the Hills, who lived in Woodland Hills. I don't remember much until about four years later when we moved to Truckee, California. It snowed a lot there. I was kind of a fearless kid, and I guess I still am to a point. At age five I rolled off the top bunk in the middle of the night and broke my collar bone. I had to wear one of those collar braces for at least two weeks. I couldn't do anything for those two weeks. That's like a death sentence for a five year-old.

My dad was a true motorcycle man; dirt bikes that is. He made my first bike when I was just a tot. It was awesome to me. It was a mini bike with a Briggs and Stratton motor on it! I loved that bike. You always love your first bike. I would pull off all kinds of crazy stunts. Soon after, I graduated to a Hodaka

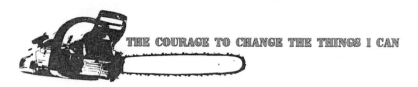

Steen 100, which was the thing to have back then. My dad had a Bultaco he used to race Enduro and a CR 250 for Motocross. There was nothing I liked better than to go for a ride out in the desert and hit the jumps even then. What a rush! I think I must have been an adrenalin junkie. Probably still would be if my body would allow it.

Lucky for me, my mom was a nurse's aide, and she was able to tend to all my daredevil induced injuries. I remember one day, we picked up a little baby boy where my mom worked. Yep, they adopted again. He was a cross-eyed baby; they named him John Hill. The eye doctors fixed his eyes, and he is fine today. In fact, he's an English teacher in Sao Paulo, Brazil and I'm pretty proud of him.

About two years after they adopted John, my parents got a divorce. From what I can remember, they were as different as night and day. They argued a lot, which I didn't understand as I was only around six. Looking back, I see that they were just too different. She was a nurse's aide; he was an artist. After the divorce, he moved to Reno. It confused me when Dad wasn't around anymore. I knew, even at an early age, that without my family, I had absolutly nobody.

We—Mom, Teri, John and I—moved to Fall River Mills, California. We moved in with my mom's family; her brother, Uncle Allan, his wife, Aunt Lillian, and their kids: Jimmie (killed in a ranching accident in 1977), Debbie, April and David. They all lived on a huge ranch. At the time, I was in the 3rd grade.

Not even a year later, we moved to Redding, California, to the Heritage Apartments on Delta Street, which are still there today. Mom enrolled us in Grace Baptist School, now called Liberty Christian, which is also still in operation to this day. I

A Convict In Training

was in the 4th grade. This school had a paddle that said "Sister's of Liberty" in big, red letters. This paddle got used on me a lot! I acted out all the time. I think I did it for the attention–I was the class clown. Also, I was a little guy, so I always had the little guy syndrome. Because of that, I got into tons of fights which I won more often than not, even though the other guys were always bigger. One more thing; it was a Christian school, and I tended to rebel against religion. One thing that I did like about school was sports. Basketball and football were two of my favorites, and I really had potential. Problem was, I couldn't stay out of trouble long enough to get to really do either.

The summer of 1975, we went to visit my dad who was now living in Carson City, Nevada, and had married a lady named Joyce. She had a son named Rick who was four years older than I was. They lived in the last house on the street. Behind them were miles and miles of sand dunes, motorcycle trails and desert. Also, there was a back road down to a market and a shopping center. There was no better way for a nine year-old kid to feel like a grown up than to ride his fancy motorcycle to the store for a candy bar!

One day Rick and I went off down the back road. We hit a straight stretch of dirt right before the store and here came a car, fish tailing and spinning right towards us. Rick swerved his bike out of the way, but he was about fifty yards ahead of me. I swerved to the left at the same time the car swerved in the same direction. So I pulled to the right, and the car did the same thing. It was getting closer and closer—almost like it was in slow motion but also in 3D. Before I could do anything, POW!, we hit head on. I went flying off my bike like a home-run baseball and landed flat on my back! The impact broke my

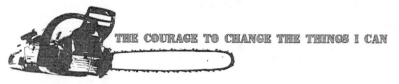

right leg. The bike was in ruins. I was in a cast clear up to my hip for four months.

Mom wasn't too pleased when I got home. As soon as I got the cast off, Pop Warner football started, and that was my favorite thing. I loved it! I was pretty darn good at it. I played middle line backer and second string running back for the Redding Colts. I distinctly remember hitting a guy like a freight train, hearing the loud clash and pop of all the pads, and not feeling a thing but honor over tackling the guy like I did! After that, I got braver and braver.

About three years later, I went to live with my dad in Carson City, and got to play football. Our team made it to the Snow Bowl in Reno, Nevada, that year. It is like a Super Bowl for kids. We won and I turned in the most tackles and sacks for the whole league.

My mom and siblings just didn't seem to click with me. They were strong Christians, and it was just something that I didn't want anything to do with. I didn't have the common decency to think about my mom's situation. She was going to college to become a nurse and was a single mother raising three kids, doing the best she could. I think it wouldn't have hurt to sit through a little Christianity. Talk about strong Christians, my mom must have gotten it from my grandparents, Benton and Dorothy Jones. Let me tell you, my grandmother was a prayer warrior of prayer warriors. She went to the grave as a very devout Christian that never gave up hope on me, bless her heart.

My dad and his family were also good Christians; his parents and sister, Aunt Helen, Uncle Dick, and my cousins, Kathy, Karen and Carol. But my dad, with his bad temper, was always much more lenient. He was a great father. We had a great re-lationship until I got into drugs. I had already been chewing tobacco for several years because I started when I was nine. It wasn't but two years living with Dad that I started smoking pot, experimenting with a little cocaine and popping speed, besides drinking every chance I got. With all this using, that was where the real trouble in my life got it's start.

Romans 10:17
"Faith comes from hearing the message,
and the message is heard through the word of
Christ." NIV

CHAPTER 2
Make A Man Outta Him

I started running away from home, and one time after I'd been gone about two weeks, two plainclothes policemen walked up on me in town and arrested me for being a runaway. They put me in juvenile hall, and I had to stay almost two weeks before they released me to my dad. About six months of this, in and out of juvenile hall, and my dad had had enough. Mom didn't want me. Dad didn't want me. I was more than a handful, alright. My dad worked for the governor of Nevada at the time as the State Planning Coordinator. He really couldn't afford to have this kind of rap. It turned out that he knew some ranchers, the Zimmerman's, out in Austin, Nevada. They had four ranches. All four of their ranches, properties and allotments were tied in together. All told, they had five and a half million acres and 20,000 head of cattle. There was The Monitor Valley Ranch, The San Antone Ranch, The Triple T Ranch and the RO Ranch. They had a ranch in McDermott as well..

One Saturday, my dad took me to a western store and bought me five pairs of jeans, five western shirts, a straw hat and a pair of cowboy boots. We loaded up the car and six hours of driving later, we were so far out in the middle of nowhere. Everywhere I looked was sagebrush—an ocean of it as far as the eye could see. We hit a dirt road that looked 100 miles long, and an hour later, we pulled up to the Monitor Valley Ranch. That's when I first met Ted Zimmerman. He was waiting for us

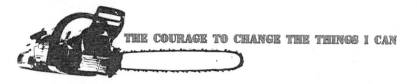

at a barbwire gate with one of his hands, an Australian fella named Steve. They payed $350 a month and room and board to regular ranch-hands, but since I was a thirteen year-old kid who knew nothing about livestock, I would be getting $100 a month with room and board. My dad dropped me off a zillion miles from no where. I was not a happy camper. I felt like he was giving up on me. I didn't know these guys, and I didn't know what would be expected of me. I was scared and angry.

I learned that the first task would be branding, and at that time, they did it the old fashioned way. Roping the calves, heeling them and stretching them out to be branded, ear marked, de-horned or castrated. We did each of the four ranches; each ranch had their own cowboys and everybody helped everybody for the branding season. We worked hard seven days a week.

When my dad came out to get me the next year, I said, "Nope. I like it here." By then I was making $200 a month and was turning into quite the hand. I liked the hard work. I liked running the cattle. I loved riding the horses. I think my dad was shocked that I didn't want to go back with him, and I think he was even a little proud that I was able to do a man's job.

One thing that was a blast was this little helicopter they bought one year to herd cattle. It was a two-seater, and it was cool because the pilot carried a pump action 12 gauge shotgun in the helicopter at all times. There was a bad coyote problem that year. Anytime he spotted coyotes, sometimes in a pack of up to four, he would land at the nearest grounded cowboy. That cowboy would hobble his horse—a technique used so that a horse can't run off—and he would take the passenger side door off the helicopter, hop in, go up and blast the coyote. I bagged at least 9 coyotes that year. In all, we killed about 50. We would skin them, cure the hide and ship them to Colorado. We made pretty good money on them. Those coyotes didn't stand a chance.

We also broke horses to ride in the winter. They would be three year old colts that had never been touched. They were wild, broncy and mean! They made me break one colt that wanted to do nothing but buck. I had to ride this horse every day, all day, and it would try to buck me off several times a day. I had to stay alert at all times on this one. It would squeal every time it bucked. They finally sold it to a rodeo company. I really liked riding the Bronc horses. I had a passion for it. I became fearless at it.

Much as I enjoyed breaking horses, I still always wanted to be high, stoned or drunk. The thing was, I got to drink all I wanted at night. I had brought some pot seeds with me to the ranch to grow my own, but it turned out I wasn't much of a farmer. I huffed gasoline when I could. I remember I always wanted to go to town on nights when the fellas went out to the bars and the brothels. I was the only kid, everyone else was a grown man. I actually got into the bars and brothels when I was just fifteen. It was a big deal for me because we lived so far out away from civilization. The only time I got kicked out was when I had too much to drink one night and ended up puking all over the bar. Being one of the fellas made me feel like a grown up. I worked like a man every day, so I was a man.

I stayed at the ranch and ended up working for each of the brothers. I outlasted everyone else that ever worked there. My time out there gave me a darn good work ethic that I still carry to this day. I got to become a good ranch hand, but after four years, at the age of seventeen, I decided it was time to move on and see the world. I got a ride into Tonopah, Nevada, and

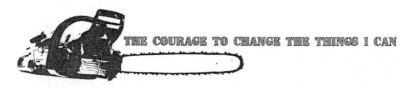
got a job a few days later—in the other direction, even deeper into Nevada. The job was for Norman and Gerald Sharp out of Railroad Valley. They paid me $450 a month and room and board, but they didn't feed me too good. I was used to eating like a king out at Zimmerman's. They had also gotten real behind on their cattle before I hired on. We were roping and heeling two and three year old bulls, having to brand and cut them, and these were some huge bulls, if you didn't know. It was hard, dangerous work.

Psalm 31:24
"Be of good courage, and He shall strengthen your heart, all ye that hope in the Lord." KJV

Mike on the ranch at 13 years old

Branding Calves at Zimmermans

CHAPTER 3
"The Rodeo Life"

I made my way back to Fall River Mills, where my Uncle Allan and Aunt Lillian still lived, and I decided to go back to school, figuring that maybe I could get my diploma. It was August of 1983. They allowed me to stay with them to go to school. They opened their home to me and did as good a job as anyone ever could have done to give me a chance. It worked out for awhile, but after being on my own all this time, I didn't take to having rules put on me. I guess I was kind of like one of those wild colts that you could never tame. Looking back on it today, they opened up their home to me, and I acted like they owed me. This particular attitude has caused me a great deal of grief in the past and a lot more than I could bargain for in the future. A selfish, all about me, my way or the highway attitude.

I wanted to play football, but it turned out that the rule books stated, at that time, that you couldn't play high school football, basketball, baseball or wrestling as an eighteen year-old. You could be on the high school rodeo team, though! How ironic is that? The high school rodeo rule book stated that you could be in high school rodeo until you were nineteen. Now, what are they trying to say about rodeo cowboys? Ha, ha! I went to my first high school rodeo as a spectator with Hardy Vestal and his sister Tammy. They were very involved in the roping and timed events. I was hooked.

Since I wasn't getting along too well with my uncle—due to my hard headedness—a girl I knew from school told me

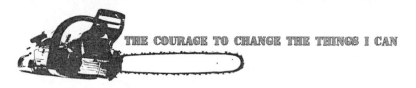
about a family that managed a ranch about thirty miles out of town. She introduced me to their daughter, Gina, who was in junior high. I asked a couple of times if her family needed a hired hand. It was about a week later that her dad came and picked me up at my uncle's and drove me out to his ranch, The Dixie Valley Ranch. His name was Rich O'Connor, his wife was Mary and their eleven year-old son was Rondo. The family took over guardianship of me since I couldn't go to school without a guardian.

I'll never forget the talk Rich had with me on the way out to the ranch. He was driving an early eighties pickup truck with a horse trailer. He told me whatever I wanted to do, rodeo mainly, that he would back me up 100% but no drinking and no drugs. I would go to school during the week and work on the weekends. Winter time at the ranch was spent feeding cows seven days a week because it snowed so deep that the cows had no grass or anything else to eat. Their water would freeze over, and you'd have to break it up with an axe a couple of times a day so they could drink. There were several sorts and types of cattle out there, so you had twenty different fields and pens of cattle that had to be tended. They had a big rig flat bed trailer that would be loaded full of about 200 bales of hay that Rich would pull with a D6 Cat to feed with and an old army 6x6.

I would drive one of the pickups to Little Valley every morning , taking Rondo and Gina, and leaving about six a.m. There was about nine miles of dirt road—or mud—depending on the season, to catch the bus. We were the first kids in the school district on the bus in the morning and the last ones off in the evening. Seemed like we were always on the bus.

Within a month, I was entered in my first high school ro-

"The Rodeo Life"

deo. I entered the bareback bronc riding and the bull riding. The high school rodeos at the time were held in Red Bluff, California, at the Pauline Davis Pavillion, an indoor arena. Rich wouldn't let me ride saddle bronc till I got pretty good at bareback and bull riding because the saddle bronc event, a lot of folks say, is the hardest event to master. So there I was, getting ready to be a rodeo rider, and the first bareback horse I ever got on blew me outta there by the 4th jump so hard that I landed in front of it, and it stomped my left hand! I still had a bull to get on. After the rodeo association rushed me to the hospital and casted my hand, I was able to get on the bull the next day. It was a little Hemsted no-horn bull they called U. I had to ride right handed, and Rich ran along side of me each jump yelling, "Hold on! Use your free hand!" And, wouldn't you know it, I made the eight second whistle! When that whistle blew, I just let go and BLAM! landed right on my head. Good thing I have a hard head, didn't mess me up at all! I ended up winning the bull riding event in my very first rodeo. I was hooked!

Needless to say, I was pretty dang cocky and full of myself, winning the bull riding even with a broken hand! Go figure, because I must have gotten on at least twenty head of bucking stock shortly after that, and I got bucked off every single one of them. Finally, I started getting the hang of things a little bit. By the next year, I was also riding saddle bronc horses. It was 1984, and I remember, because of point standings, I qualified to ride at the famous Cow Palace Jr. Grand Nationals in San Francisco. It was a dangerous situation there, loading the bucking stock in to the bucking chutes because they had to run the bucking stock right by all the cowboys while they were getting ready to ride. A big ol' horse ducked back and ran an old man over, I mean hit him like a freight train. My horse was loaded in the chute, and I was next to ride. Talk about wanting

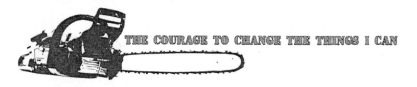

to lose your nerve! I toughed it out, but the Cow Palace was weird because the grand stands were packed full. The only light was a spotlight shining on the current cowboy and the event at hand. I got on my bronc, got set, nodded my head, and they let him out. Right when the eight second whistle blew, my front and back cinch broke, and I landed in the dirt-still in the saddle. Funniest thing you ever saw.

Guess what? I won 3rd place! I also won rookie of the year. The O'Connor family was a rodeo family like you've never seen. We would all go on a little two or three week tour in the summer time, hitting every Jr. rodeo there was. Between Rondo, Gina, and myself, we won money and buckles darn near everywhere we went. I stayed with them for a few years.

Phillipians 4:13
"I can do all things through Christ, who strengthens me." NKJV

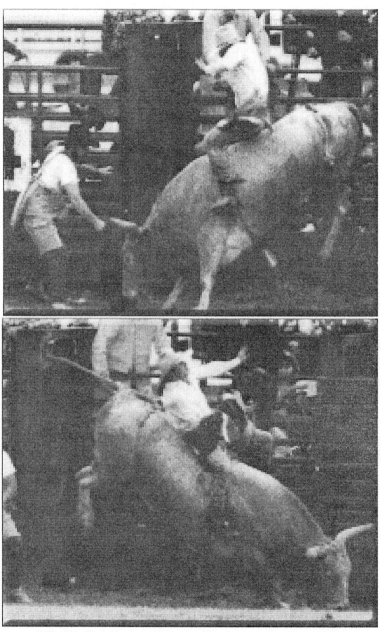

Mike Bull riding at Booneville CCPRA Rodeo 1985

Mike riding "Dunngone" 1985 McArthur CCA Rodeo

Mike riding "Ugly" 1987 at Oregon House, CA

CHAPTER 4
Job After Job After Job

In 1986, I found a job at the Shasta Livestock Auction Yard in Cottonwood, California. I moved out there because I wanted to be in an area that I could get on bucking animals every day of my life. Cottonwood had just the climate for it, being much warmer in the winter than where I was from. There just so happened to be a man by the name of Don, who was putting a rodeo company together. While talking with Don, I asked if he had any roughstock I could get on. He told me to be down at the arena by 5:00 that afternoon, that he already had a few guys that wanted to get on something. Maybe, if there was one extra, I could get on a little something, too. Well, I showed up. They had six bulls and four guys. They loaded up the bucking chutes. All the guys got on all the bulls with no horns—the "gentler" looking ones—ha ha! But no one wanted the big, ol' snorting Brahma with the three foot long tusks coming out of his head; no one except little ol', crazy me! I got on that bull and many more after that—and lots of buckin' horses as well for quite a few years. That was a beautiful thing. I not only got on bulls, but I rode all three roughstock events.

Don had a few partners, Jeff—who is the sole owner of Four Star Rodeo Company today—Ronnye, Billy and Cody. These guys must have wondered where in the heck this little cowboy came from. Twice a week they would have anywhere from six to ten animals for me to get on; whatever they could

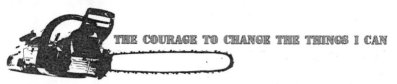

get their hands on. I'd get on one, hop or get bucked off, jog back, get on the next one, and just keep going like that. Sometimes there would be a couple of other guys getting on a few, but, me? I was hungry for it. Pretty soon, Don was calling me Yeager. Chuck Yeager is a famous test pilot for NASA. The nickname stuck. I became known as Yeager all over the rodeo circuit. Some people still call me that to this day.

They also had a great bullfighter named Donnie Martin who saved the skin of a lot of bull riders. A bullfighter's job is to save the bull riders when they come off the bull and land on the ground. Donnie was one of the best. However, he had an unfortunate accident in June of 2008 and passed on that July, bless his heart.

What I really need to say goes back to my addiction to drugs and alcohol. I had laid off the meth during this time in my life—for about a year anyway. But I would fall asleep drunk as a skunk each night. I was bumped to night shift at the auction yard, feeding cows. This one particular night, I drank a twelve pack of Shaefer Beer. That is some broke cowboy beer right there. I crashed the feed truck into the back of an old flatbed. The feed trucks got abused up there; often they didn't have lights. I wrecked the truck. It hit so hard that it crushed me into the cab, no exit. I broke my leg up pretty good. A few days later, I'm down at the arena tryin' to get on a bull or two and Andy, one of the owners of the auction yard, fires me.

It seems like, through my early life, different families would take me in. I mean, I didn't always ask, but I guess that a lot of people I came to know would know that I had no place to go and would take me in. My family didn't really want me because I'd shut them all out through the years with my drinking and using and my ways. I started living with Bob Edwards and his family about that time. Their house was on auction yard property, not even 200 yards from the rodeo grounds, so I was content. Bob was a horse shoer who worked at the auction yard a couple of days a week. We really hit it off. He admired the fact that I could get on more bucking stock than anyone as well as my talent and my love of the sport. But I remember the little lectures he'd give me about saving myself a little bit, and that I'd be lucky to be walking and talking when I turned forty. I wouldn't listen, though. Wish I would have listened now, I'd be in a lot better shape.

I just got fired from the auction yard, and I needed a job. One thing about me, I could always find work. I got a job in Anderson, California, at a veneer mill. I worked there during the week, got on animals after work and went to rodeos every weekend. This was Four Star's first season and the other rodeo company, Hemsted Rodeos, was also out of Cottonwood. I was pretty much in with them as Dick Hemsted was the owner there. He used to give me a ride in the stock truck and pay my motel and my rodeo entry fees, to do a little thing called the Wild West Show at the beginning of the rodeo, right after the grand entry. It consisted of the guys running an old, gentle saddle bronc. They loaded a bucking horse named Chicken George into a bucking chute. Everybody wanted to draw this horse because he was gentle as a puppy, but he could buck! They would let Chicken George out of the chute, and a rodeo clown, Dan McNair, and I would put my bronc saddle on him. Meanwhile, the rodeo announcer would be explaining the early days of bronc bustin' while we were doing all this. Then, I'd get up behind Dick Hemsted on his horse and he would ride along side of Chicken George. I would then get my feet in the stirrups of my saddle, Dick would yank on the flank strap, and Chicken George would get to bucking. Thing was, I had to jump off, making it look like I got bucked off for the crowd. So

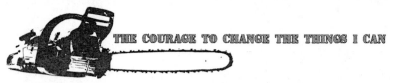

this little gag became known as the Wild West Show, and the crowd always loved it. It paid my entry fees for a long time.

Four Star also did the same thing. They had a pinto horse owned by Jeff for theirs. I've got to mention another well known rodeo cowboy, like myself but much more successful. His name is Harley. He is probably the only other person that ever got on as many bucking animals as I did, but he won quite a few more rodeos. However, his rodeo career ended in the 90's sometime when his head and a bull's head met head on. He wasn't the same for a long time, but I see him from time to time. He seems to be doing pretty good.

I must admit that going from rodeo to rodeo every weekend, sometimes two rodeos in a weekend, is not only a lot of travel time, it's a lot of wear and tear on the body. Add to that my drinking, smoking pot a lot and snorting a little bit of crank (methamphetamine). All this wear and tear caused me to do more and more crank. Before long, I had to have a snort of it just to function. That was around 1988, and I think I was living at the Cottonwood Rodeo Arena. Don always had a place for me to stay. I don't think they really even knew about my drug use. But when addicts become addicted to their drug of choice, they are in such denial over their disease that they think they can hide it well. Addiction of any kind is a disease. I didn't think of myself as an addict yet, but I was bad, looking back on it now.

Psalm 3:3
"But you, O Lord, are a shield for me, my glory, and the lifter of my head." AMP

Mike riding "U" High School Rodeo 1984

Mike riding Jason f-13 CCA Rodeo 1990

CHAPTER 5
What Happens In
Vegas Stays In Vegas

My dad and I had made contact. I don't remember how. It had been years. He was the general manager for a tour bus company in Las Vegas, and he sent me a check to buy a bus ticket to come there. He was going to get me a job as a mechanic's helper. I had nothing else going on at the time except my drugs, and rodeo season was done for the year. I told my good friend, Justin, about it, and I'm not sure if everyone was just trying to get rid of me, or if they really thought it would be good for me. Instead, I bought an 'eight ball' of crank with the bus money. Thinking like an addict, I thought I could just get high and sell the rest of the dope, making my money back. Unfortunately and predictably, I did the whole bag myself.

Keep in mind, I still didn't think I was a drug addict or that I even had a problem. A few weeks later, I still wasn't in Vegas, and I don't remember what lie or excuse I gave my dad as to why I wasn't there yet. So, he mailed me a bus ticket. A few weeks later, there I was, on a bus, headed for Reno and from there I would hop on another bus to Vegas. I met a dude on the bus who seemed pretty cool. He was headed somewhere else after Reno. We both had a twelve hour lay over in Reno so we put our money together and bought a huge bottle of Jack Daniels. We took turns hitting the bottle and by the time I got on my Vegas bound bus, I was tore up. Last thing I remember was asking a pretty lady across the isle from me if she wanted

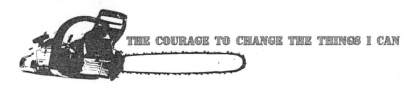
a drink off the bottle. I don't know what happened, but I woke up in jail in Hawthorne, Nevada. The next day, when I woke up, they were getting ready to transport me to Reno 'because I had warrants for 'minor in possession of alcohol' a ticket from years ago that I had never taken care of.

There is nothing like a father's love. Thanks to Dad, I made bail right after getting booked into Washoe County Jail and was back on a bus for Vegas. I finally made it there in one piece. What a site that city was! Here I was, a country boy from a little Northern California town, thrust into a seemingly never ending sight of bright lights; yellow, blue, green, red—all kinds as far as the eye could see. My dad was there to pick me up at the bus station. He never said a word, although I could tell he was thoroughly disgusted with my traveling performance.

The next day, he took me down to work and introduced me around the charter bus company, Western Coach Service, owned by Vern Williams. The bus company was in a run down neighborhood in a real bad part of town. I stayed with my dad at his little studio apartment for about a month until he moved to a condo in a nice part of Vegas.

All I could get my hands on was alcohol. It seemed that crank was unheard of there, and that's what I wanted. I did, however, manage to get introduced to someone from work, who was a major marijuana connection. However, every time I wanted a bag of weed, I'd have to buy the guy some shrumstick, which is a form of liquid pcp that they make into a cigarette and then smoke. It is such an intense high, that you feel like you can fly. The first time I ever tried it, I met up with the dealer and had to give him a ride to his house. I could smell the pcp odor real strong. It smells like some type of insecticide. He lit it up while I was driving and passed it to me and WOW! I immediately thought the little pickup I was driving was flying. I remember we were on a long, straight desert road in between some busy traffic streets. It was at least two miles long, and I was hallucinating so bad, I thought I was flying an airplane! Thank God we didn't wreck.

Needless to say, I didn't much care for the shrumstick. But it wasn't very long before I had my first taste of crack cocaine, and crack was the closest thing to crank I could find in Vegas. It was a very intense high that only lasted about fifteen minutes. Crank would keep you going for days. The reason I'm talking about all the drugs is, this really became my life, which led to a downward spiral. This is the same for any addict. You hit rock bottom sooner or later. The end result will always be a devastated life, spiritual bankruptcy, institutions, jail, homelessness and death. That's a fact!

I would get paid every Friday, and there for awhile, I'd think nothing of blowing through $250 on crack in the course of a weekend. I'd buy thirty dollars worth at a time. The sad part is, I could smoke that up in an hour or so and find myself driving around looking for more an hour later. Crack was plentiful in Vegas, you can believe that. People stand on the street corners with it in their hand; it's a drive up sort of thing. I even got mugged one night. I was stabbed in the ribs over a deal gone bad.Even with all this, I still didn't think I had a problem.

I got in a fight with a bus driver one day down at the shop. Everyone watched. There was an old bus driver they called Jazz who saw the whole thing. Next thing I knew, he introduced me to an ex-heavyweight contender of the world, named Leroy Caldwell. I don't know if you've ever heard of him, but he was the biggest man I'd ever met—around 6'6" tall, as wide as

a rhinoceros, weighing around 275 pounds. He fought Larry Holmes two times and lost to a decision both times. He was pretty well known as a trainer when he took me in and trained me. I was never serious enough about it, though. I didn't eat right, smoked my stuff, and drank. I trained for a few months. It never turned into anything, but we remained friends.

Proverbs 21:23
"Whoever guards his mouth and tongue, keeps his soul from troubles." NKJV

CHAPTER 6
Family Reunion

My life's dreams always played second fiddle to my addictions. There were a lot of things I really could have been great at, and that's why "having the courage to change the things I can"is what I go by today. Two years after getting to Vegas, I moved back to Cottonwood and back into a trailer at the rodeo arena. Thanks to Don, I always had a place to go. I lived there for six months to a year, I don't really remember. I rode a few colts for Bob Jones and fed the rodeo animals for my keep. They held all the high school rodeos there at the time. One day, I ran into Rondo O' Connor. I hadn't seen him in years. He was riding and roping and everything. This kid was real good, let me tell you.

I got offered a job with a logging company. At the time, I was going out with Barb, sister to some of the fellas I rodeod with. I met her at a bar in Cottonwood. She was a little older than me, a lot shorter than me and, with her long blond hair, a whole lot cuter than me. I left the arena, and Barb and I and her son moved into an apartment in Anderson. We moved in together almost overnight, much too quick. I found that I loved logging. I started shearing trees. The shears are big machines that just pinch the tree off at ground level and lay it on the ground for chipping. I was still drinking myself to sleep every night, smoking pot at work and snorting crank whenever I could. Barb would drink with me, but she didn't like any of the other stuff, so I had to hide that.

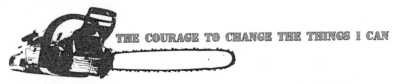

We all know that relationships don't work when dishonesty is involved. It took me many more years to learn this. Every lesson I ever learned, it seemed, I learned the hard way. I was too much of a drug addict for Barb, and we split up less than two years after we got together.

I was working on the aftermath of the infamous Fountain Fire Burn. That burn provided about five years of work for every logging company around. Since I wasn't living with Barb anymore, I needed to find housing. I moved into the Travelers Motel in Cottonwood for a decent weekly rate. It wasn't long until I was actually intrigued by a maid working there. Her name was Gerri, and she cleaned my room daily. She wouldn't leave me alone. She would make me breakfast of eggs, bacon and toast and bring it to me every morning about 3 am, before work. We got to know each other a little bit. What was interesting was that she was here illegally from Nova Scotia, Canada. She came to the U.S. on a trip to Corona, California, and never got on her return flight home. Somehow, she ended up in Cottonwood with a job as a maid through a friend of a friend she met in Corona. She had bought a little Datsun, but she had no license or insurance. I used to give her a hard time and say she had defected to the U.S. She was also very naive. It wasn't too long until I got Gerri pregnant. As a surprise, I rented a nice, cozy little apartment down the street. A great friend, Scott Deburger, gave me some furniture for it. We got it all ready, and I went to the motel to pick up Gerri. Just seeing her face light up thrills me to this day.

We lived there seven months when, lo and behold, on July 12th, 1993, Gerri told me that a lady called who said she was my mother. She asked questions and knew things only she could have known. She said she'd call back at 6 pm. She told Gerri that I could talk to her if I wanted; if not, she would un-

Family Reunion

derstand. 6 p.m. rolled around, and the phone rang. Of course I talked to her! I had so many questions for her. I had always wondered who she was, what she looked like—all sorts of questions. I had questions about my birth father as well. We had a great talk. It turned out she had spent three years trying to find me, even hiring a private investigator. I would never have looked for them because I always figured I hadn't been wanted. I had a lot of wonderment about the whole thing, and I am so grateful that Bob and Deanna Hill, my adoptive parents, told me the truth about being adopted.

This whole thing had Gerri kind of nervy and wouldn't you know it, her water broke a couple of hours later! After eighteen hours of hard labor, she gave birth to my first son, Justin Michael Hill, on the afternoon of July 13th, 1993. He had long, bright red hair; it was good looking hair, too. So I actually got a mom and a son on the same day. What a blessing. Gerri had a very difficult labor. Poor little Justin was born with a black eye and abrasions on his little face. On top of that, he had swallowed some embryonic fluid during the birthing process. They had to stay in the hospital for a week, but we all made it through.

I started forging a relationship with my mom from there on out and got introduced to my father over the phone when he called me. They split up not long after I was born. My mom remarried in the early seventies to Jeff Dunn. They had a daughter, Megan, my little sister. My dad had two kids with his lady: Chris, my brother, and Nikki, my sister.

It wasn't long before Gerri wanted me to marry her, so we got married in August, 1993. It still didn't make her a U.S. citizen, like she thought it would.

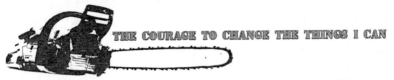

Time went on, and around December, I got laid off for the winter. That's no big deal for loggers—we all got laid off every winter. It was the perfect time to see my mom. Once I got down to see her and spend some time with her, she arranged for me to drive her car down to Huntington Beach to meet my dad. So, off I went to see him only to find out that he walks around with a cigarette pack with about twenty rolled joints in it daily. I wanted to see Hollywood so that evening, he drove me there. On our way, we stopped off at his friend's place. His friend was a biker. We walked in the house, and he had a Harley Davidson Motorcycle taken apart on his living room floor. My dad scored some meth, and you know that was a bad idea. Both of us wound up wanting to talk at the same time. Neither one of us could get a word in edgewise. It became a big mess. Needless to say, we didn't get along too well, and it's sad to say the drugs got in the way. I only saw my dad one other time after that, and we got in a big fight. I haven't seen him since.

The next few years went by with me logging about nine months out of the year. I was working for another logging company now. In those years I was unbelievably strung out on meth. I couldn't function without it. But I prided myself on never missing a day of work—up at 2 am, if I slept at all, and home by 7 pm. On December 18, 1995, we had another son, Winston Gerald Hill. I don't remember his exact measurements, but he was much smaller than Justin. I remember he got deathly sick with pneumonia and jaundice but made it out of the hospital in two weeks.

It wasn't too long after Winston Gerald was born, that my mom and my sister came to visit for a week. It was sometime in February and I was off work. I always used to cut firewood in my time off. I was so strung out, I stayed gone cutting wood the whole time they were visiting. I know they were very dis-

Family Reunion

appointed in me. My mom had been clean for quite a while now. It caused some friction between us, and we didn't speak for a couple of years or so. The only time I would call her was when I wanted to borrow money for drugs. What a shame, looking back; not only to borrow money, but to have it sent by Western Union, and right now! How selfish and thoughtless. Using addicts don't care about putting someone else out, or anyone's feelings, as long as they get their next fix. I'm so grateful to know that today.

About September 1996, I got a call from Mary O' Connor. She informed me that Rondo was just coming out of a coma. He met head to head with a 2,000 pound bull in a rodeo. He was in Redding Rehabilitation Hospital. He didn't really recognize anyone and she wanted me to go see him. I remember trying to make myself look as presentable as possible. I brought Gerri and the boys with me. When I walked in, Rondo was sitting in the cafeteria trying to eat. He couldn't even feed himself. I walked up and stood there. He looked at me with a blank look on his face. Then he mumbled, "Mike Hill". It was so hard, I had to fight the tears, but it gave me hope that he would be OK. I hung out with him for about three hours. We thumb wrestled, and I let him win every time. When we left , I didn't see him for a long time because of my addiction.

2 Timothy 1:7
"For God did not give us a spirit of timidity,
but a spirit of power,
of love and of self discipline." NIV

Mike's First meeting with his Birth mom Kathi,
she is holding Mike's son Justin

CHAPTER 7
The Logging Years

The winter of '96 proved to be a tough one. It was an El Niño year, and no one was logging. It rained from December until May, non-stop. Cutting firewood was even getting tough. It had rained so much that I got my truck stuck in the mud almost every day. Even the seasoned firewood was soaked clean through. But somehow, the good Lord allowed me to provide for my family; to enable us to survive.

One day early in May, I was looking through the help wanted ads in the paper and came across one that said 'hook tenders, rigging slingers and choker setters needed'. I jumped on that, but it was a 707 area code. I called and asked it they needed timber fallers and the guy told me to get over there. It turns out that area code 707 is the California Redwood coast. This job was in Mendocino County, in a little tourist trap called Gualala. The first thing I did was find enough meth to last me awhile since I didn't know a single soul where I was going. After that, I got my saws ready, threw my clothes together and left my family at home. I drove all night to get to a job, scarcely knowing where I was going.

I finally made it at daybreak—to a rude awakening. All the country over there is almost straight up and down. The job was for a company out of Coos Bay, Oregon, called Tri Tower Logging. A tower, in logging, means a yarder; a piece of logging equipment which uses a system of cables to pull or fly logs from the stump to the landing. This yarder was different

from what I was used to. It involved flying the timber out of steep canyons and mountains with the use of miles of cable strung across the canyon one or two hundred feet in the air. I had to learn to cut timber for a yarder without anyone knowing I was learning. Cutting on a yarder job, you have to throw all your trees 'side hill'—that is, along the side of the hill—so they won't slide top first all the way to the bottom which could be up to 600 yards. You can't make money chasing your trees to get them cut into logs, but if they are side hilled, you can actually walk the tree as you cut the log to preferred lengths. You always start at the bottom of the hill and work your way up so that any possible loose log that could roll, is down below you. It is quite dangerous. They payed their timber fallers by scale, so you got paid by what you accomplished. They were paying $17 a thousand, which means $17 for every thousand board-feet of timber you cut. You had to cut at least 15,000 board feet a day, but you aimed for 20,000. To the average cutter, that sounds easy, but I gotta say that the steep terrain was so unbelievably steep that if you happened to set your water jug down wrong and it started to tumble, it would roll clear to the bottom, and it would be the leg workout of a lifetime just to get it back. You had only six hours a day to do your cutting. Timber fallers the world over generally only work six hours a day because it is such a physically demanding job, it gets even more dangerous when you are exhausted.

You have to know I was spun out of my mind when I got there. After working that first day, Kurt, the owner of the company, put us all up in some old, junker trailers that night. Trying to fall asleep, I prayed to God to keep me safe, even though I never talked to God in the past. I think he was watching out for my safety because he kept me alive through my wild and crazy rodeo days as well as all through my logging career. I am convinced He has always watched out for me because he has a purpose for me. I'm learning what it is.

I worked for two weeks, got some money and headed home to get my family and more crank. I'm sorry to keep mentioning that, but that was my life. The thing was, cutting timber and snorting crank just went hand in hand for me. I got back home to Redding, we packed our stuff and stored the rest at my old friend, Tim's house. My family and I just disappeared to the coast. I had moved the trailer up the North Fork of the Gualala River, off by ourselves. Everyone else was on the Southfork. I called it the riff raff camp. So I went to work every day, and it wasn't long until I found someone local to supply my habit. It always seems that someone can find what they are looking for in the drug world no matter where you live. It's become such an epidemic.

We camped out for six months before we got a house that we could rent for the right price. The money was good over there, but the cost of living was absolutely outrageous. All Gualala was, was a little tourist town that had a highway running through it. It was only about 1.5 miles long. Every pay day we would all pile into Gerri's station wagon and drive the two and a half hours to Santa Rosa to do our laundry and buy saw supplies.

Proverbs 14:23
"All hard work brings a profit,
but mere talk leads only to poverty." NIV

Mike in his logging Machine.

"Chainsaw" Mike doing his thing.

Mikes first wife and two sons on top of a
Giant redwood that mike cut down.

Mike and a Big Sugar Pine

Justin, Winston & Mike with one of the
giant redwoods, that Mike had cut.

Chainsaw Mike with a Giant Redwood
that he cut down.

CHAPTER 8
Losing My Wife And Kids

About two years after we moved there, I got a DUI on my way home from work. They towed the car fifty miles away to Elk and took me to jail in Ukiah. I got out the next morning, hitchhiked to the car, and finally go home by night. The bad thing was, the highway patrolman that gave me the DUI worked the Gualala area a lot. Now I had to drive all the back roads to and from work. That man pulled me over and towed my truck three times before we actually moved.

It was late February, 2000. I had just got my unemployment check since we were all laid off due to weather. We all loaded up and disappeared just like we arrived. We had to. It had gotten to the point where we couldn't go anywhere. We ended up back in Cottonwood. At this point, Gerri was really starting to hate my guts. Looking back, I don't blame her one bit. I had singlehandedly endangered all of their lives. Because of my addiction, she lost all faith, trust and respect for me. Looking back, it just breaks my heart, the things I did and places we had to go because of my selfishness. But I have been forgiven by her, and most importantly, the Good Lord.

We ended up, of all places, back at the motel where Gerri and I met. We had enough money to stay there for a week, so I had to find some work. The motel was only 500 yards from the auction yard where I used to work, and they needed someone on the feed crew to feed the cows on the graveyard shift. I

took it. I made enough money for us to stay at the motel and enough to eat, just enough to scrape by. But we'd been scraping by all the while; I knew no other way. And when you have a drug and alcohol habit like I did, that's all you're going to do until you spiral even lower in life.

Gerri kept threatening to leave me. She told me that one day I'd come home and they'd be long gone. All this behavior of mine affected my marriage because I was not the man she thought she was getting involved with at all. She would harass me to no end about being loaded or drunk all the time. That led to me not being home very often. I didn't have a lot to do with the boys, either. When I was home, we wrestled and played and such, and I thought we had a good relationship. But the sad fact is, I was never myself. I was always loaded. I went to work loaded and came home and drank myself to sleep if I slept at all. If I didn't sleep, I would be tweeking in the garage all night, messing with my saws or working on my truck. Whatever it was, it was not something needing done, I was just tweeking.

I knew she was homesick for Canada, and I could see that I had turned this sweet, vulnerable lady into a hateful, miserable, negative person. The problem was, I didn't care. When you're as addicted as I was, you don't care about anything. That is why you see so many kids getting taken away by CPS (child protective services). Usually, it's both parents caught up in the disease of addiction and these poor, innocent lives are completely neglected. I thank God to this day that Gerri was not an addict or alcoholic. She was probably the best mother I've ever seen.

But things got worse around September of 2000. She told me that she and the boys were going to Canada. I had just gotten $5,000 back on my income taxes. She got airplane tickets

Losing My Wife
And Kids

and passports for the boys. I had just landed a timberfalling job with Watkins. I gave Gerri $2000 to get them to Canada. I spent $500 and bought a new saw. She had me go to a notary and fill out a permission slip to take the boys to Canada. She had all her i's dotted and her t's crossed. She was not kidding at all! She told me to go ahead and stay here and that I was welcome to join them at Christmas, if I wanted to. I got up at 3a.m., September 17th, 2000 , the day they were leaving, to say my good byes and give the boys hugs and kisses before going to work, not knowing that I wouldn't see them again for many, many years..

Justin was now six, Winston was four. I called two days later because that was how long it took them to get settled. They made it safe and sound. After that, the connections by phone got more and more scarce. Not that I didn't call, but Gerri made sure that she and the boys weren't available. The sad awakening for me was, although I was strung out like I was, I was suddenly all alone. This, in turn, sent me deeper and deeper into my addiction. Pretty soon, I only called once a month and could never get ahold of anyone at all.

Psalm 25:16
"Turn thee unto me, and have mercy upon me;
for I am desolate and afflicted." KJV

Justin, Winston and Mike in there little house on the coast. "Note how strung out I was."

"One of the last times I ever saw my boys."

CHAPTER 9
Meeting My Soul Mate

Sometime in October, I was at the drug dealer's house, and lo and behold, a little cutie, 5'2" beauty named Shaleen showed up. Through the years, I'd really had a thing for her and her for me as well. We had known each other for about ten years or so and had always wanted to hook up, but couldn't because I was with someone or she was with someone. But, hey, now we were both available! Let me tell you, it was on!

We were both drug addicts, so, at the time, it was great. I didn't have to hide my use from her, and she didn't have to hide hers from me. I was living in a little duplex in Cottonwood. I'd been layed off. Shaleen had a job working for a spa company. She would come by my house in the mornings to do a little dope on her way to work. But, you see, she used the needle, and let me say, people, the needle is a terrible thing. In fact, I would tell her I didn't want to see it. If she wanted to do that, she had to go in the other room. I didn't believe in it. That was one step further than I wanted to go.

I was cutting firewood full time now. Within a couple of weeks, Shaleen quit her job and started helping me cut wood. She came and stayed at my house, leaving her daughters at home with her parents. Her oldest was Lacey whom I'd seen around for years. She was in the eighth grade. Kacey was 4. Shaleen comes from a big family and the reason she is so tough is, she grew up with three brothers. There was Charles, Rod and Brian, and Shaleen was the youngest. She had to grow up tough. Her mother and father, Pat and Darrel, would

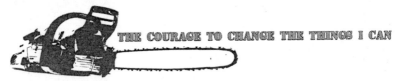

always take the kids when Shaleen was out running amuck. It was a blessing in a lot of ways, Gerri taking my boys and Shaleen's parents taking her kids. We would have surely lost them to Child Protective Services the way we lived our lives.

Our son was born in August. Jayce seemed to be a happy little guy, always smiling. However, we found out a few months after he was born that he had problems. The doctors diagnosed him with cerebral palsy. He has no use of his right hand today. It stays like a claw but he has become most talented at dealing with what he has. Between Shaleen's parents and her brother, Charles, and his wife, Wendy, they had Jayce a lot for his first year. Shaleen and I were too far into our addiction to be able to care for him.

It wasn't long before I took my addiction over the edge— off the cliff to where there would be no turning back—and that was when I started using the needle. Once you start doing that, there is no turning back. Besides it being dirty, it becomes an addiction in itself. The high is so much more intense; you're putting the drug directly into your bloodstream. It gets to where you will do anything in the world for it. It becomes your god. They say meth is the devil's drug, and it is.

Now life, besides the drugs, had become even more of a strain on our relationship. We got to the point of hating each other. We would fight to the point that all the windows would be broke out of my house. She would take off, or we would both disappear for a few weeks. We always missed each other deeply when we were apart. That's how I knew we were meant to be together.

Meeting My Soul Mate

Psalm 69:5
*"O God, thou knowest my foolishness; and my sins
are not hid from thee." KJV*

Shaleen Barrel racing at age 9

Shaleen with my saw on an allnight firewood trip.

CHAPTER 10
The Life Of Crime

Four months into my needle use, I started burglarizing, strong arm robbery, home invasions, whatever it took to feed my habit. So, if you look at my life, I went from a somewhat honest, hardworking young man to an animal and menace to society, in that order. The landlord kicked me out of my house, and I had no where to go. I found myself living under the Cottonwood Creek bridge. My drug dealer had given me a huge tent that I set up under the bridge. That was Mother's Day weekend 2001. Shaleen at least had a home, although her parents made her sign over custody of the kids. She would stay with me once in a while. When her parents left for work, she would take me there and feed me since I wasn't allowed out there.

I would burglarize at night and sell the stolen items to the drug dealers. That was how I lived. Sometimes Shaleen would help me, but I would almost have to force her, and it wouldn't even be worth it because we would go to fisticuffs over the merchandise. But she had the car. Nothing like seeing a burglar packing his loot on his back at daybreak, which I did quite a few times. A couple of months went by, and a guy in town let me put my tent in his backyard. They called him pops. His was pretty much a drug house.

I had schemed up this idea about doing a strong arm robbery on a local grocery store. I always had burglary tools on me. They consisted of a crowbar, a flashlight, a couple of screwdrivers, a lock back buck knife with a 10" blade—just

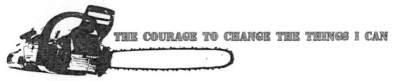

plain deadly. I'd already rummaged and found a shirt that was three sizes too big for me, and some bib overalls, also too big for me, to throw off any physical descriptions of me. Shaleen and I were in the tent one night, and I told her about the job. She said "no way!" To my clouded mind, it was perfect. Have you ever heard of the perfect crime? There isn't one, I'm here to tell ya.

This grocery store had been the same since I was a little kid. They pushed all the shopping carts up to one of the entrances on the west side of the store, and only used the east side after hours as they were open twenty four hours a day. What gave me the idea was that I had been up there two weeks prior and right by the east side doors they had a flower shop set up inside that had a cash register right by the doors. I almost grabbed the register then, but I was on my bike. I don't know how heavy a cash register is, but my odds of getting away packing one would be about the same as putting a Shetland pony in the Kentucky Derby. I noticed that all the workers stocked all the shelves at that hour and no one worked the regular store registers, so that's when I got the idea. A burglar alarm had gone off an hour prior to me seeing all this, and I noticed that it took the Police Department about ten minutes to get there. Plenty of time to pull off a robbery.

Psalm 30:3
"O' Lord, thou hast brought up my soul from the grave: thou hast kept me alive, that I should not go down into the pit." KJV

CHAPTER 11
Bonnie And Clyde

So here I am in the tent, trying to talk Shaleen into this, and I had to come short of threatening her very life to drive the getaway car, which also had to be push started every time as the key didn't work. I suited up in the wee hours on June 13th, and we pulled into the parking lot of the store to check out the scene. I had her pull two full blocks away and park, listening for me to come running. I had taken a set of her pantyhose, tied a knot in the leg, pulled it over my face, and walked into the store. I was awfully nervous but dead set on going ahead as this stunt was going to be my only chance at more drugs. That was my only reason for doing it; well, that, and because I'd gotten away with all the other stuff, so I had a false confidence built up.

I stormed into that store, got to the register in the middle of the long row of registers and, sure enough, all the workers were stocking shelves. I stuck my crowbar in, pryed, and POW!, the register opened! It was full of cash! I started stuffing my pockets. Just as I got them full of about $600 in fifties, twentyies, tens, fives and ones, I heard a thunder of feet running right at me! I pulled the knife up and roared like a lion! They all back-pedaled with their arms in the air as I ran out the east side doors, just as planned. As I ran off, my heart was pounding like the hooves of stampeding buffalo. I heard footsteps follow me for about a block. I couldn't believe it when I got to the car. I ran and pushed it to get it started and we were gone like the wind. Little Shaleen can drive, let me tell you. I don't

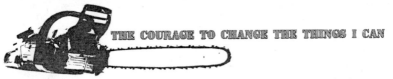

remember much about the rest of the night, but I do know that we paid the drug dealer what we owed and got more.

You know how they say that the first time you do something like that is the hardest? And after the first time it gets easier? Well, they are right. You get more gutsy and careless, and you're bound to get caught sooner or later. I had another job in mind, so two days later, in the wee hours of the morning, I hit a grocery store on the other side of town. Only this time, I had the car parked on an incline for an easier push-start. I got in the store, and there was a lady mopping all the little aisles between the registers. So, I popped open the first register I came to and it rolls open... empty! The lady hadn't looked up. I storm right over to her, knife in one hand, crowbar in the other. She looked up when I approached her, and I said "what cash register is open?" She almost screamed, but she held her composure and said number seven. I even said thanks. Sure enough, as I was done stuffing my pockets, she got on a loud speaker screaming for help. As I got to the sliding exit doors, they didn't open automatically as they normally would. I had backed up a little for a running start to run right through the glass when it whooshed open! This time, the footsteps only chased me for a short distance, and as I got to the car, Shaleen had the trunk open, all the doors open, stuff out of the car on the ground. I screamed at her to get in the car as I neared, and we barely got going, but we made it.

I have to say, we were pretty messed up kids. That was insanity at it's finest. My addiction had now opened a door from which there was no going back. I couldn't undo what I'd done. There was a homeless guy sleeping in the bushes, and when I came running to the car screaming, he saw it all. I found out later that he gave the cops my license plate number. We got on out of there and headed straight for the casino. Shaleen

Bonnie And Clyde

and I both agreed to make this our last hoorah and check into rehab. We got a motel room. The room key they gave us was the wrong one, and as we were trying to open it, the door opened from the inside by a couple with kids inside. I'm sure that raised a few red flags. We got in our room finally. We were both so very beat up and burned out that we fell asleep. I think we had been up for about 21 days or so.

Sometime, early in the evening, we both got startlingly awakened by a very persistent, loud knock on the door. I heard the distinct sound of a long, metal flashlight whacking the wooden door Thirty or forty times, and then, "Mr. Hill, this is the Police Department. We need to talk to you." I got up, my heart about ready to explode out of my chest, and I slowly crept up to the window, looking through a crack in the curtain. I could see at least six policemen, half of them in dress suits. Shaleen wanted to open the door. I whispered to her, "Don't open it." In fact, I snuck up and slid the little security chain in place—as if that would save me. They knocked and beat on that door for twenty minutes straight, and then the phone rang. No way were we answering that. I looked cautiously out the back window. The whole building was surrounded. I don't know why they didn't kick that door down, but they did slide a business card under it with a detective's name on it, and just like that, they were gone.

Three hours later, we bagged up all our stuff, went out looking everywhere, no sign of a cop or anything suspicious. I push started the car, and we pulled out. Within two miles, we had an undercover on us. I kinda slid down in my seat and told Shaleen to lose them. Boy, she did pretty good weaving in and out of traffic; left lane, right lane, left lane, right lane. We took a side street, and were just three cars ahead of them. We pulled into a shopping center, hit a dead end, and that quick, as we

tried to make a turn around, two of them had us boxed in like a drop of honey on an ant, guns drawn, yelling, "Hands up!" I kept dropping my hands. Both of us were telling each other goodbye, just knowing we'd never see each other again. The first cop got to my door. I felt the solid steel barrel press up against my temple with total authority. They got me out of the car first, leaving Shaleen. It was around 110 degrees, and the pavement felt hot enough to fry an egg on. They got me in the prone position, face down on the pavement, arms out on my sides, their knee in my back.

As they tried to cuff me, there were only two cops. I distinctly remember saying to myself, "I'm not going out like this!" In one motion, I was up on my feet, one punch knocked the cop trying to cuff me on his back. Then, I was off and running. The problem was, my burned out mind was telling my legs to run faster than they ever possibly could have run. I kept getting myself tripped up but I made it to the fence, which was six feet tall and wooden. I was just getting over it with one cop pulling at my shoe strings. I jumped another fence, and another, and another! Then I buried myself under a huge redwood tree. In the meantime, they had left Shaleen there while chasing me, so she got away.

It wasn't but ten minutes and that whole neighborhood was swarming with helicopters, sirens, voices and dogs. They were combing that area for 15 minutes before I saw the cop that I had knocked off me. He yelled, "There he is!" and boom!, I was up and running. Right when I got to the fence, two young rookies hit me from behind. We went right through the fence, smashing it into pieces. They proceeded to beat me with a baton until they layed me open. I was caught.

I basically came to handcuffed and strapped to a hospital bed, with two plainclothes detectives questioning me about

66

Bonnie And Clyde

the robberies and asking me where Shaleen was. I told them it was all me, all me. She turned herself in a few days later since we were all over the news, but I took the whole rap for it. I think when I got to the jail cell, I slept for two weeks straight. Court dates started in about three weeks, and they came at me with ten years at first. I had no money, so I got a public defender. I didn't take the ten years, and then they offered me eight years. I was new to all this deal stuff, so I had every convict in my jail pod trying to tell me what to do.

Shaleen came to my court appearances. All she could do was give me the love sign in sign language. It gave me hope to see her face because I loved her so. At my fourth court appearance, I took a deal of two years, eight months at eighty-five percent. That meant that I would have to do eighty-five percent of my time; no half time because it was a violent crime. I also had to take a 'strike' because it was a violent crime. In California, if you get a third 'strike' you are in prison for life. There is no getting out again. So there it was. Shaleen and I got married in the jail with the big window separating us, on July 16th, and at 4 a.m. on July 18th, they came for me to take me and fifteen others to state prison.

Joshua 24:15
"Choose for yourselves this day
whom you will serve." NKJV

CHAPTER 12
High Desert State Prison

It was early afternoon by the time everyone was dressed out in orange jumpsuits, belly chains, ankle chains and handcuffs. They scrunched us all into a County Sheriff's van. I happened to be in the rear facing backseat, and I could watch my hometown of Redding disappearing for what, at the time, seemed like it was going to be forever. I kept telling myself, "Mike, you deserve every bit of this."

Two and a half hours later, we pulled up to the first twenty foot tall cyclone outer perimeter gates of High Desert State Prison. California Correctional Center (CCC), was on the other side in another tall, cyclone fence. All fences had rolls of the infamous razor wire strung out on top for what seemed like miles. We got through the gate and three correctional officers, (CO's), scanned the van. One had a mirror on a stick to check under the van. We went another mile or so, going deeper and deeper in to the waiting lion's mouth.

Reality was setting in; I wasn't feeling so tough now. They finally pulled up to the R&R side of the building; and, no, R&R doesn't stand for rest and relaxation. It stands for Receiving and Release. Six CO's were waiting, and they pulled us out of the van one by one and drilled us. The process is, they have a picture with your paperwork. "Hill, birthdate- 6-7-66". As soon as you hit the door, there's another CO stripping you; the whole

bend over and cough routine. Then everyone gets thrown in one cell, like six hogs in a one-hog pen. They take you one by one, fingerprint you, interview you, and ask you if you have any known enemies on the yard. After about six hours of this, they finally line you up and walk you in one long line, one cop at the front of the line, one or two in the middle and one or two at the end. It is another half mile to your temporary home for the next three to four months. Welcome to reception!

There was a prison car driving back and forth on the outside of the fence as we made our way, just waiting for someone to get stupid. The twenty foot cyclone fence with razor wire was now also electrified with a sign every forty yards saying stay back, electric fence, 50,000 volts. We finally entered the cell block, and I'll never forget it: a huge, gymnasium sized block with two tiers on three sides, wrapping up in a half circle. There had to be two hundred cells with convicts yelling out of their doors, while some were jogging in place, looking out of the six inch wide by two foot long window in the middle of their doors. It was just total commotion. I admit I was scared, but I knew I deserved what was coming to me, and I was going to hold my head up high and take it like a man.

The whole prison was on lock-down because a convict had stabbed a female CO the week before. They sent me to cell 238, and I was now a number, T-22531. I'll never forget that number. God was looking out for me again, because they bunked me with an older dude that had done this little trip a hundred times. Over the next four months, he schooled me and prepared me for the yard when reception was done.

I wanted to go to the fire camp like I kept hearing about, but I also heard that there was no way they would ever let someone with my convictions, out the gate to a conservation camp. In September, I got validated for CCC, the prison next

High Desert State Prison

door, which is a firefighter training center. Again, it took all day long to get the handful of us that went ready. I hit the Cascade yard that evening. The second you walk on to the yard, you're considered a 'fish', which is what the convicts call a new commitment. The yard reps of each race are convicts who get you segregated to break down the rules of that particular yard: this is the Black's area; this is the southern Mexican's spot; no smoking with other races; whites stick with whites. If a riot breaks out, you help your race even if you weren't involved. That's how it is in every California prison. Luckily, it turned out I knew quite a few of the fellas there. All of Shasta County goes to that prison, and it was pretty much run by Shasta County.

This was all dorm living, and it was the most depressing place I had ever been, even to this day. I was surrounded by two thousand convicts, but I felt so depressed and alone. I think it was because Shaleen hadn't written to me in months. I missed my two sons badly, and my other kids, too. The reality of my messed up life was really getting into my head. I finally got a letter from Gerri, and she told me that she would continue to throw any letter I sent in the garbage where it belonged. This was the one and only letter she would ever send. However, she sent pictures, and I think that was to make me even sadder. While I clung to those pictures, I didn't look at them too much because it hurt so bad to think of my two sons clear on the other side of the continent. Ten years later, it still hurts me.

Psalm 39:13
"O' Spare me, that I may recover strength,
before I go hence, and be no more." KJV

Mike's mugshot from his second
time in.

CHAPTER 13
Fire Camp

December of that year, I got cleared to go to fire camp. That lifted my spirits a little. I had to pass physical fitness training (PFT) and it was December in Susanville, California. This meant lots of snow when I started PFT. To pass this, you had to do calisthenics all day long under the direction of a coach, who was the local high school football coach. He came in every day with a stop watch. You had to run a mile in under eight minutes every day for a week. Coach would document your time each day. Under eight minutes for a week classifies you as a (((HOG))). If you couldn't run it in under eight minutes for a week straight, you had to keep doing it, week after week, until you could. Some guys did their whole time in PFT, never making it to camp. I was a HOG the first time.

A few months later, they authorized me for fire fighter training, FFT. For that, you get transferred out to Arnold Unit. That process would take two more months. It was a lot better than the yard. The food was better and you could move around a little more freely. They put you on outside work crews. Certain CO's would take crews out to do different jobs in the community. There was no chance of escape in a fluorescent green jumpsuit in a town that is ninety percent populated by the CO's that work in the two prisons. FFT was a two week course which you had to pass. If you failed, you had to start PFT all over again.

The system wasn't going to stick someone out on a fire unless they were in shape and had at least a little knowledge of fire fighting. During this time, my grandmother, Dorothy

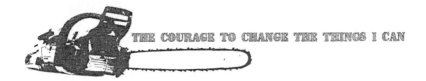

Jones, died. She was the prayer warrior that never gave up on me. I got word because they called me into the program office to tell me. It hit me mostly because of where I was. I was realizing that all these things were happening on the outside that I could never change. Oh, what I would have done to be able to sit and listen to her preach to me now; especially since I never cared to hear a word of it before. I would never again hear her ask me if I was saved or read a Bible passage to me.

So here I was, mid-December, running my tail off on a frozen asphalt track going HOG status and on that Thursday afternoon yard, all of a sudden, a riot breaks out. Two hundred southern Mexicans were all running across the yard towards a huge gang of northern Mexicans. Complete chaos! Stabbing, kicking, and punching went on for ten minutes. The cops up in the towers started shooting their mini-14 machine guns. There was tear gas; sirens were going off; stray pellets were flying; and gunfire was going on overhead. I was just hoping I didn't get caught by a stray bullet. Everyone in the whole yard was down flat on the ground, as is procedure when the alarm goes off. Needless to say, the whole prison was going on lock down for two weeks after that. Two weeks later they kept the northerners on lock down because everytime they came out, a riot would break out.

The group I was in for PFT had to start all over again. I felt that I would never get to Arnold Unit. I did though, two months later. After that, I graduated to FFT and was finally in a camp in March. There are approximately twenty eight inmate fire camps in California from way up north to clear down south. I have no idea how I slipped through the cracks of the system by getting to go to camp with my crimes because I, by rights, should have had to do the whole sentence behind the walls. I only did about a year and a half inside on that sentence. I end-

Fire Camp

ed up doing eighteen months at Delta Conservation Camp in Suison City, California, just outside of Fairfield.

Fire fighters make one dollar per hour on fires, which doesn't sound like much, but it adds up. We fought many fires in Southern California. Shaleen was pretty much doing the same old stuff we had been doing before I went away. I'd get letters a week straight, then nothing for months on end. I never got anything from my boys, which really hurt. Although I was in a better place, I still had lonelines and emptiness in my heart that I just couldn't explain. I did get loaded now and then. I tried heroin for the first time at camp. The sick thing was that it was a worn out needle someone had come across. After they hit me with it, there were about twenty guys waiting to use it after me. I must say, "Thank you, God," for me not liking heroin. I did it that one time and never tried it again. But speed? That was entirely different for me.

The fire captains loved me because they had never seen anyone with the saw skills I had. In fact, "Chainsaw" became my nickname and still is to this day. I'm only known as Chainsaw to a lot of cops, fire captains and convicts. . Most don't know my real name is Mike. At Delta, I met a dude named Red Dog. Mike Tickner is his real name. He was a great saw as well, and we ended up on the same crew. He was also from Redding and we just clicked. We are best friends to this day. However, he has made a career out of being a convict. We were great friends from the get go until he got in some trouble and they rolled him up to another camp. We've stayed in touch through the years.

The one and only visit I ever got was my little sister, Megan. She came out to see me one time. They never approved Shaleen as a visitor since she was my crime partner.

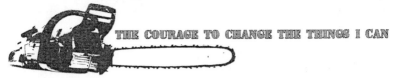

When it was six months to my release date, I was transferred to the camp kitchen so I could try to get my mind right for the streets. All I had to do was clean the tables after morning and evening chow, and mop the dining hall floor. One day I got called into the camp office. My grandmother that passed away left me $5000, bless her heart. I was a month away from release, and the lieutenant put the check in my lock box for my release. My birth mom, Kathi, sent me some parole clothes, and Shaleen's mom did also to be sure that I'd have something to wear other than state issue parole clothes. I'd made the whole parole plan; I had logged in 1700 hours worth of fire pay. I really wanted to do right when I got out. The statistics say that the recidivism rate for parolees getting reincarcerated is ninety percent.

I came up five days 'to the house', as they called it, and an old warrant came up for my arrest in Tehama County, for a possession of marijuana charge that I never took care of. Do you see the madness and insanity associated with the lifestyle? I found myself on the big green bus with bars on the windows headed back to Susanville and the CCC. Needless to say, I didn't parole on my date. They kept me in the Sierra yard gym for a week before the Tehama County van came for court people to go out for charges. They chained us all up; ankles, belly chains, handcuffs. The officer driving told me they would try to cite me and release me when we got to Red Bluff, if we made it there on time. Luckily, they weren't too busy as it was Friday afternoon. Man, I wanted that little van to go so fast as it could, all the way down the hill.

Proverbs 16:3
"Commit to the Lord whatever you do, and your plans will succeed." NIV

CHAPTER 14
WWW- World Wide World

Two and a half hours later, we rolled up to the Tehama County Jail. It wasn't thirty minutes until they had me dressed out in my street clothes. Boy, did that feel good after three years of wearing bright orange. They shoved me out the back gate of jail, back into the big wide world. That quick, there I was standing on the street with a garbage bag, with all my personal belongings slung over my shoulder. I was out on the street with cars flying by; the whole world was flying by. What a weird feeling, and I had only been gone for three years. Could you imagine the feeling of being flung out after ten, fifteen or even twenty years? All the changes in the world? So, there I was. The first thing I knew I had to do was get to Redding, get a motel, and hide out until morning when I would report to parole.

I wanted to do right; I had the desire but I found myself at a store buying a six pack of Budweiser and getting on a pay-phone. I had gotten the beer without even thinking. Hadn't I learned my lesson? Didn't I wanna stay free? I had a problem, and even though I didn't know it, the problem was me. I hitched a ride to Redding, got dropped off at a cheap motel about a mile from the parole office, bought more beer, and began to drink. I tried calling Shaleen, but her mom didn't know where she was. We hadn't talked in months, Shaleen and I. So I had a steak dinner at a Bar and Grill and got a little drunk. It didn't dawn on me until the next morning that I had to give a urine test to my parole officer within twenty four hours of being released.

I paid for everything with my $200 gate money every convict gets at their release. I still needed to cash my fire check and my grandmother's inheritance check. I chugged down about a gallon and a half of water and luckily scathed by that test. The afternoon of my first full day out, Shaleen's mom located her at a drug house and brought her up. When she got out of the car, I didn't even recognize her. She weighed eighty pounds at most and looked just plain beat down. That moment, right there, I just wanted us to get right and stay right. She had sores on her from head to toe. The kids were with them, but they couldn't stay with us until we could show we could responsibly handle them.

Shaleen gave me a huge, desperate hug that I'll never forget, and I hugged back happily despite the sores because I loved her so. I told her mom that we'd be ok. She said, "Huh. We'll see." I had full plans for taking off in life like before I went away until I saw Shaleen in the sorry state she was in—and the kids. Right then I determined to stay clean.

My sister, Teri, helped me cash my checks the next day since all I had was a prison ID. After a couple of weeks at the motel, I decided I needed something to do. Parole was on me to get a job, and I kept seeing logging trucks heading through town. I started calling the logging company I used to work for. Two days later, they sent the crummy (the crew pickup) to pick me up at the motel since I had no license or vehicle. Right away, they had me running a Timbco feller buncher. I would cut logs in the morning and skid them with the cat in the afternoon. It was awesome. I think the boss understood, as he had a son that went to prison a few times.

Life was good for a while, except I still drank my beer every night. This would not be a problem for most people, but it sure is for an addict. It released the gates of my addiction, which I didn't realize at the time. It wasn't but a month, and I talked a realty company into renting us an apartment in downtown Redding. I had all that fire money and inheritance money. We moved in, and things sure seemed good. Shaleen stayed clean, also.

Winter came, and our job moved up to Poison Lake near Susanville. The big boss had me cutting the bigger trees with a saw since there wasn't enough timber to go out and hire a timber faller. I would cut in the mornings and skid the logs I cut with a cat in the afternoons. He told me he'd make it worth it for me, and he did. He gave me a brand new saw for doing the cutting and we had winter work for once.

Ephesians 1:3
"Praise be to the God and Father of our Lord Jesus Christ, who has blessed us in the heavenly realms with every spiritual blessing in Christ." NIV

Logging Camp

Shaleen at our logging Camp

Mike bucking a log he cut

CHAPTER 15
Too Much
Holiday Spirit(s)

A different guy was picking me up to catch the crummy now. He was also on parole, and his name was Dennis. It was Christmas Eve, the crew had dropped me off at my cutting spot and it was snowing and blowing that day. Trucks couldn't get in, so the boss called it quits at 11 am. Our foreman bought each of us on the crew a half gallon of Christmas brandy. So, here it is, Christmas Eve, payday, going home early! I started hitting the bottle before we even got to the pavement. By the time we got back to Redding, I was a blackout drunk. My ride was drunk, too. After we got to his truck, I don't remember a thing until we rear ended a car at a stop sign. I almost went through the windshield headfirst. As soon as we hit and I realized what happened, I yelled, "Go!". He hit reverse, and BLAM! we backed into another car! He hit drive again, and we were in the ditch, stuck. I jumped out, and two parolees in a van pulled up saying "You need a ride, Bro?". I dove into their van. I don't even know how I gave them directions to my apartment. We pulled up, I jumped out and ran for home. Shaleen was all dressed up in Mrs. Claus garb. I was covered in blood. I don't even know what I told her, but within ten minutes, helicopters were buzzing the apartments, and twenty patrol cars were pulled in. The Police Department pulled me out of the shower and put me in cuffs. I woke up Christmas day in jail.

A week went by, and I didn't hear anything from anybody. My parole officer was on vacation and it was up to him to figure out what to do with me. I denied to the bitter end being drunk. Two weeks later, my parole officer came. After a half hour of pleading, he reluctantly let me go home.

The logging owner was fuming mad but he let me keep my job. Dennis went back to prison because of the DUI, parole violation and hit and run. The job finished up a month later, and we got laid off for a while. One day, I rode the bicycle to the store to get a a newspaper; or so I said. I actually wanted to get the paper and guzzle a 42 oz beer, which I did. Riding back, I got hit by a car going 25 mph at an intersection. All the traffic stopped, and I tried to run, but I couldn't. I tried to ride the bike, but I couldn't as both wheels were folded in half from the impact. I had to get away before the cops came. I barely made it, carrying the bike over my shoulder and hobbling. I finally made it home. It would have been a one year parole violation for sure.

The readers must be asking, is this guy nuts or just plain stupid? But, please bear with me. I think you'll like how things turn out.

Psalm 13:3
"Consider and hear me, O Lord my God:
lighten mine eyes, lest I sleep the sleep of death." KJV

CHAPTER 16
When I Finally Realized
I Had A Problem

It turns out I cracked my hip from that little stunt, so I was layed up at home for the next three weeks until our next job started in Weed, California. I still didn't have a vehicle, but the log company owner had a trailer that Shaleen and I could use during the week to stay up there. I bought a little Ford Bronco just to drive off road as I was cutting timber again. Shaleen's mom would drive us up every Sunday night and pick us up every Friday afternoon, so we could come home on the week-ends. We did this for several months until the job ended in June.

When we got layed off, I had $2,200 cash in my pocket. One day, Shaleen tried and tried and tried to get me to buy a $50 bag of dope, and I'm not blaming her because I could have said no, no and no! But, you can guess, I finally gave in. As soon as that poison hit me, I ran with it. I thought I could buy $200 worth of it, sell it off and make money. Folks, it doesn't work like that with me. I did all $200 worth. Back we went, out of control, both of us. It was sad to think, being off drugs, we loved each other so very much, but on drugs, we hated each other. We just kept doing this to each other, to ourselves and to our families.

Thinking back, I even kicked the door of a neighboring apartment in one time because I knew that the people living there had some dope. They didn't like Shaleen and I because we were way too crazy and scary for them. I kicked in the door

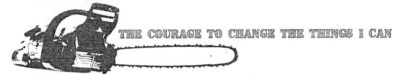
with my little Shaleen by my side, and there sat an Asian gang, guns and all. We must have put the fear into them because they didn't even move. We took their dope. We were a scary couple, let me tell you! I think the clouded mind of drugs made us feed on that.

Right towards the end of the cash flow being sucked dry, my homeboy, Red Dog, started coming around. He had dope. I remember sitting in the living room of our apartment with the spoon in my hand waiting for a handout, watching him put his in a glasspipe, waiting, watching, waiting... That was when I realized for the first time ever that I had a problem. I was an addict. Something clicked in my brain that the only thing that was going to make me feel better was when someone finally put a piece in my spoon so I could go do it. That's when I realized I was sick. But I didn't know how to do anything about it.

Romans 3:23-24
"For all have sinned and fall short of the glory of God, being justified freely by His grace through the redemption that is in Christ Jesus." KJV

Red Dog & Chainsaw

CHAPTER 17
Shaleen's Overdose

About that time, I was called in to the parole office because I had given a couple of dirty tests. I had to walk three miles to get there. My parole officer interviewed me a little bit and warned me that if I gave one more dirty test, I was going back up the hill to High Desert for a year. When I got home, Shaleen and I got in a huge fight. She was at the point that she didn't even want to live anymore. When I wasn't looking, she swallowed a handful of pills. She waited to tell me about it after they started taking effect. I didn't know what to do. She got to the point where I couldn't keep her conscious, and I was afraid to call 911 as I might get booked for it. I walked her around; I put her in a cold shower. Her eyes turned like a cat's eyes with the pupil being oblong shaped, up and down. It was scary. I did this, keeping her awake for three hours or more, and as soon as I would let her sit down, she would go unconscious. I finally put her on the bed and was able to wake her up every 10 minutes or so; however, she was not the least bit coherent.

All of a sudden, a knock came at the door. I was so paranoid, I answered the door. It was my parole officer doing a sneak check on my house. He started talking kind of loud, and I said, "Shhh. My wife's sleeping." He looked around a little bit and left. I couldn't believe I made it through that.

I finally got Shaleen stable enough in the next couple of days to live, but she was very, very sick. I finally took her to the hospital, and they kept her on IV's for a week or so. She lost most of her left kidney from the overdose. We made it

out of that, and a few weeks later we were loaded and fighting again so the cops were called. It's funny how, when that happens, your house becomes empty; Shaleen left. Dummy me, I stayed. A whole fleet of patrol cars showed up. The cops came through the door and Shaleen showed back up. I had what seemed like the whole department tearing my house apart. They found a lock back pocket knife on Shaleen's side of the bed in a bowl on the night stand. Even though Shaleen claimed it, they took me. I had a really rude awakening the next morning, sitting in the Sheriff's van, shackled down and headed back to High Desert.

A month later, the parole board made a decision to give me five months straight. I couldn't believe it. I thought I was going to do at least a year so I was pretty happy. I ended up doing a lot of my time on the level three yard with lifers. There was a lot more prison politics and convict rules. You wore your boots to the shower in case a race riot kicked off. It was a lot more serious.

My release date was December 12th, and at the end of November, the prison showed the movie, "The Passion of the Christ", which I walked out on after ten minutes. I mention this because even though it had no impact on me at the time, it would play a huge part later in my life. I finally made it to a lower level yard. I finished my time there and was paroled on December 12th, 2004.

John 8:36
"So if the Son sets you free,
you shall be free indeed." NLT

CHAPTER 18
For Old Time's Sake

Shaleen's mom and brother, Rod, picked me up. Rod is also a meth addict. Rod, Shaleen and I are the only addicts in the whole family. The others all lead the straight and narrow life. So, I got out, and Shaleen didn't come because she wasn't able to travel. She was beat up again from the drugs; again weighing in around eighty pounds. I had the $200 gate money and bought a weeks worth of motel for Shaleen and I. Again, we couldn't have the kids; we weren't capable. I said and did the dumbest thing possible, I told Shaleen, "Let's get high one time and put it down forever." She didn't want to. I kept bugging her and bugging her. She still didn't want to.

You see how the vicious cycle goes? I can't explain it to this day. A real monster had gotten in to me. All I wanted to do was get high. The drug life had turned me into a convict. I thought like a convict. I wanted to be a convict. We did our thing that night, and, bless Shaleen's heart, she put it down. I didn't. I kept sneaking it, lying about it, hiding it. All the while, Shaleen stayed clean. When the motel money ran out, Shaleen's oldest brother, Charles, and his wife, Wendy, and daughter, Jackie, let us come and stay in a camp trailer at their house in Cottonwood. We stayed there for three months; the whole time, I was sneaking dope.

Shaleen talked her dad into loaning us $2000 to move into a beautiful, A frame house about two miles from Charles and Wendy. It was on thirty acres and had a double wide trailer that our daughter, Lacey, and her boyfriend could live in. It

was perfect for all of us, and the kids could stay with us. We had horses as well, so it was good.

I went back to work for the logging company. However, I just couldn't shake the dope habit, while Shaleen stayed absolutely clean, which was a miracle. We fought a lot over me being loaded. I came home from work on my birthday, and I walked into the house. There was a trail of rose petals leading me into the kitchen. There stood Shaleen, waiting for me. I was wired and high. That just totally broke her beautiful heart; it broke her down. You see, an addict can only be around someone who is using drugs just so long, , before they end up falling off the old, reckless wagon.

Psalm 119:11
"Your word I have hidden in my heart that I might not sin against you." NJKV

Mike limbing a log at Poison Lake

Shaleen in her
Mrs. Claus garb.

CHAPTER 19
I Got My Drug Partner Back

I came home the next night, and Shaleen was high out of her mind. That's all it took. She came back with such a vengance that she called my boss and told him I was on drugs. My boss kept me working under the understanding that I would take random drug tests. It didn't matter. I kept using. I'd stay awake for long periods of time, and I mean weeks at a time. I was just a walking, talking zombie with no sense of reality. It got so bad that I would fall asleep during the day running logging equipment, and I'd come to while the machine would be in motion. How dangerous is that? Funny thing was, no one ever noticed.

Each Friday would come, and I'd tell myself, "OK, I'm going to sleep all weekend." Then I'd find myself with a bag of speed in my hand before I even realized what I had done, and before I knew it, Monday would be there. One day, the woods boss came up to me at about 1:00 pm. to have me take a random test. I told him I'd never pass a test, it hadn't been long enough. Needless to say, my check was waiting for me when we got down the hill. I didn't even care. I was so messed up and arrogant, I told them I'd be working for someone else by the end of the week.

I went home and partied even harder for a few weeks before landing a job cutting timber for another outfit. I had the

91

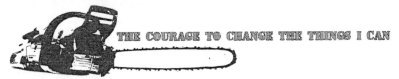

disease of addiction bad. I was using Lacey's '93 Chevy pickup to drive to work each day. I had been working for these guys for about a month. We were working in Oak Run, and Shaleen and I would party with friends all night. I would always take off around 3:30 am and head straight to work. It was an hour and thirty minute drive. I took Shaleen to work one day and we were late. I made the trip in 45 minutes flat with Shaleen putting on makeup on the drive. She didn't even look too bad either.

Isaiah 7:9b
"If you do not stand firm in your faith,
you will not stand at all." NIV

CHAPTER 20
The Wreck

I headed to work on July 25th, 2005. Shaleen had thrown some food in my lunchbox—like I was really going to eat it—along with a 40 oz bottle of beer. At the end of the day, I guzzled that on the dirt logging road before I hit the pavement above Oak Run as I headed for home. After driving down the highway 5 miles I nodded off for a second and Wham!, I hit a huge cedar tree, head on, doing 65 mph! That woke me up. My panic reaction was to climb out, which I could not do. I was crushed in the cab. The steering wheel was underneath me; both my feet were bent backwards under the seat; and the drivers side door was wrapped around me! I was hurting like nothing I've ever felt before. All I could do was try to scream. As I've said about God looking out for me, He was because the tree I hit was right in front of someone's house. There wasn't another house for miles and miles, and the guy was home. He came out and kept telling me not to get out because there was no way. Also, the truck was hot and leaking oil and gasoline. He dialed 911 and then Shaleen. All I could do was sit there, twisted up like a pretzel, yelling, "Aaahhhhh!!!".

This went on for twenty minutes before the fire department got there. They couldn't get me out either. I was wrapped up looking like I was wearing the truck for Halloween. The fire department had to call for the jaws of life from a town twenty-five miles away. The whole incident had traffic backed up for miles in both directions. Forty-five minutes later, they cut the truck into enough pieces to get me out. A hospital helicopter landed and flew me out of there.

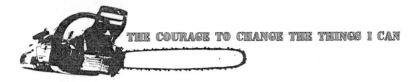

Was God looking out for me? Think about it. They took me into emergency surgery to save my left leg. My left femur was broken in five places from the knee cap to the hip. I now have a long metal rod and lots of screws holding my leg together.

A highway patrolman came to my hospital room the next day to give me a ticket for no seat belt. Can you believe that? I'm lucky I didn't get a DUI. They kept me in the hospital for two weeks. Shaleen's family all came to visit, but they sure weren't impressed with me at all. Plus, I had totaled Lacey's truck. The doctor's said I would be lucky to walk right again. In fact, Shaleen's mom was so furious with me that she hit every speed bump at about twenty miles per hour on the way home.

We made it home that evening, and my drug dealer came by to check on me and offer me some dope. For the first time in my life, I turned down drugs—free drugs at that. That is until the guy kept asking me over and over, not believing his ears because Mike Hill never turned down a drug. Sadly enough, I gave in. Here I had two weeks in the hospital off my drug. Now I started it all over again. I'm the kind of addict that once I start, I can't stop. I know that today, thanks to God above.

The next couple of months went on like they always had. We got kicked out of the house. The kids went back to Shaleen's parents. Then Lacey gave birth to a beautiful baby girl, Montana Lynn. Shaleen and I weren't even around. We were now grandparents, but we were still deep in our addiction.

Along about September, we noticed the school buses on the country roads in the morning picking up kids for school. School had started, and we weren't even there for that.

94

The Wreck

Psalm 6:2
*"Have mercy upon me, O Lord; for I am weak: O Lord,
heal me: for my bones are vexed." KJV*

CHAPTER 21
Please, God, Don't Let Her Die!

On October 15th, 2005, Shaleen and I got in a huge, drug induced fight over some stupid thing I don't even remember. We were at a drug house, obviously, and she hit me over the head with a bottle. When I went for her, the doberman pincer that lived there would bite my leg. I had Shaleen hitting me and a dog biting me. She got away from me and proceded to overdose again and left to go die, as she put it. It was dark, and everyone was trying to talk me into going and looking for her. I had been up for so very long that everything I looked at in the dark was a hallucination. I said, "Let her die," even though, I didn't mean it. A half hour had passed, and all I could do was call some friends that had a drug house up the street, to drive down the road to see if they could find her. They found her, alright, upside down in a ditch completely unconscious. She was dying. All we could do was call 911. The paramedics arrived shortly and they started working on her. They worked on her for what seemed like an eternity. Everyone was waiting for the verdict. The paramedic that was pumping her chest and shocking her with the paddles got no response. Finally, he just stopped, got up and looked at me and said, "Michael, I'm sorry." I screamed and fell to my knees crying out to God not to take my wife, praying, "God, please, please. I'll change, I'll change my life!"

Miraculosly, Shaleen's little heart started beating, and they

started working on her, stabilizing her. All of a sudden the roaring wind and bright lights of a medical helicopter pulled in and landed in the field right there. The paramedics got her stable enough, and off she went. My drug friends had a beat down, old car with no brakes, bald tires and no gas, but we found enough change for gas and rushed to the hospital.

Shaleen was in a drug induced coma for three days, unconscious with machines and tubes and wires keeping her alive. Just standing over her, watching her fight for her life, I made a promise to myself, to God and to Shaleen that I was going to change. If she made it out of this, I was going to take the first step and get myself some help. I did the last bit of dope I had in my pocket over the course of the next two days, watching her. It seemed to be the only way I could handle it. When the last bit of dope was gone, on the evening of October 17th, 2005. I stole a syringe from the very hospital she was in and took it to a bathroom. The syringe was defective. I told myself, this is it, I'm done.

I started October 18, 2005, drug free. Shaleen was stable enough to go home on the 19th, but we had no home. Charles wife, Wendy, had been at the hospital on and off since Shaleen was admitted, and they let us stay with them temporarily. My mind was set to stay clean above all else. As hard headed as I was, I knew that this was it. If I stepped back out into hell again, I'd never make it back. I would end up with my 3rd and final strike and do a life sentence in prison—or I would die. Plus, Shaleen had just been sent back by God for one more chance as well.

I slept out in their garage for the next week, recuperating and trying to call all the recovery facilities in the area with no chance of getting in because they were full, or I didn't have

Please, God, Don't Let Her Die!

enough money. I also thought that parole was looking for me since I hadn't checked in in quite a while but found that I had been put on write in's. That's where you just simply mail in a monthly report of how you're doing, where you are living, and so forth.

James 2:17
"Faith by itself, if it is not accompanied
by action, is dead." AMP

A beautiful view from logging camp in Weed, CA

Lacey, Mike
Jayce, Shaleen
and Kacey

CHAPTER 22
Keeping My Promise To God

I finally kept bugging and harassing a friend of mine that used to be in the game with us, who was now a drug and alcohol counselor at a recovery facility in Red Bluff. I really had to bug him to let me in. I didn't have much money, except for my disability check twice a month for my broken leg. He reluctantly pulled some strings for me and got me into the next best thing, which was a sober living house in Red Bluff for $300 a month. It had some requirements; I had to go to at least three Narcotic Anonymous or Alcoholic Anonymous meetings a week, I had to sign in and out whenever I went anywhere, and I was subject to drug tests whenever they wanted.

I was so proud of myself when Shaleen's mom dropped me off there because I spent my disability check on something good—my first month's stay—instead of blowing it on meth. I also had to enroll in Drug and Alcohol classes. First, I must say, I did everything that was asked of me and more. I was determined to succeed at staying clean and sober. I programmed myself to go to the 11:00 am meeting every single day, the 7:00 pm meeting every single night, and my Drug and Alcohol classes three afternoons a week. It was a one year class.

I was determined to get my first thirty days clean. You get a different colored key chain each thirty days that you stay clean, and the first one was bright orange. I had never had

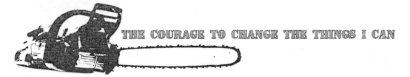

thirty days clean off any drug or alcohol in my life, so I had my eye on it every day, as it was so very important to me.

I looked a mess when I first showed up at the meetings. I only weighed 150 pounds. I had at least fifty needle marks going up my arms and legs and I was on crutches, if you want to call them that. Shaleen had Barry Bond's me over the leg with one of them in a fight, so it was beat up. The other crutch had been so abused when I was on drugs that it had no cushion for the armpit piece, a stick made to fit for the handle part, and no rubber skid boot on the bottom. I thought no one would notice I was messed up. Hello! They knew all right! But they welcomed me anyway. Thus, with my heart set on doing this recovery thing wholeheartedly, and determination, and a desire to be successful, I finally got 30 days clean!

Shaleen was still recuperating at her brother's place, and the kids were staying with her a lot, which was a good thing. Charles let me borrow his pickup to drive to the meetings. Charles is an avid hunter and fisherman, and I was so pumped and excited to be going to get my 30 day chip that I didn't even pay attention the fillet knife on the dashboard and all the bullets of all kinds rolling on the floorboard. Just as Shaleen and I were pulling up to the first stoplight in Red Bluff, the light turned yellow. It was a fast yellow, too, and turned red when I was 3/4's through it. Wouldn't ya know, right there to pull me over, was a highway patrol car. I jumped out to steer the cop away from the knife and the ammo, and I just started in, "Officer, I'm sorry. I'm in a hurry to go get my 30 days clean chip." I lost my driver's license somewhere before I got clean, so all I had in my possession was my prison ID which he took and looked at. He knew I was a parolee, as we tend to have the look, but he kindly handed the ID back to me without even looking in the truck and said, "Go get your chip."

Keeping My Promise To God

I'm positive if Red Dog had been with us, the truck would have gotten ripped apart, but he met us at the meeting. Boy, did I have a story to share. I can't say early recovery was a walk in the park because it wasn't. I not only had to stay completely clean from all mind altering substances, but I also had a lot of work to do on the inner me. I had years and years of emotional baggage to deal with. I had all these feelings coming up that I had never experienced before. The drugs had always kept me from feeling them and this was very different. They say that a person's mind actually stops growing when they start using, so I actually had the mentality and emotions of a teenager. In addition, I was carrying around my prison mentality as a 'tough guy' type of mask. I was still a mess, but I was clean and sober, and that was a start—a huge start for me.

Psalm 18:28
"For you will light my lamp; the Lord, my God, will enlighten my darkness" NKJV

Shaleen & Mike living Clean

CHAPTER 23
Living The Recovery Life

I remember the first couple of times I called Justin and Winston in Canada. All I could do was cry because I was so disappointed in myself and felt so sorry that, because of my actions, addictions and selfishness, they had spent the last six years without their father. Kids need parents, both of them. The thing that weighed on me so heavily was that there was no going back. Seeing their first day of school, their first hockey goal or even their day to day routine, I had missed all that and could never recapture it. Just the thought of it crushed me.

In my opinion, past emotional baggage is the single hardest thing to deal with in early drug treatment: those we hurt, those that hurt us—it was all my fault. Yes, it is painful, but it never gets better until we go through the pain, deal with the pain and work on a solution. Time is a great healer of pain, both physically and emotionally. So the solution is getting time put together in the real world, not some narcotic induced fantasy world where nothing is real except the next score.

One of the first things I did in Red Bluff, along with recovery, was join a gym. My whole thing was getting healthy, and when I got to this point I only weighed one hundred fifty pounds. My cheeks were sunk in, and I'm talking about all my cheeks. I was very sickly looking. It's true that meth = death. My daily program became; up at 5 am, eat breakfast, hobble on the mending leg one mile to the gym, then workout un-

til ten a.m., hobble to the NA meeting at 11 a.m., go back to the sober living house, eat, then sometimes go workout again, and finally go to my afternoon and evening meetings. My gym also had a physical therapy department, so disability helped pay to have my leg rehabilitated.

Two months into recovery, I bought a little beat up pickup for two hundred dollars. I noticed that as long as I stayed clean, things actually started getting better. They say it's called "Living Life on Life's Terms" which is exactly what it is. I had lived out of a bag of dope or a bottle all my life, never living life according to it's terms and conditions. I lived according to how I was going to get my next mind altering substance because I didn't want to be in my own skin.

One evening, Shaleen and I borrowed the movie, "The Passion of the Christ," from someone. We watched the whole thing through and something happened to me that night. I watched this man, Jesus Christ, the Son of God, being punished beyond recognition; whipped, beat, spit on, a crown of huge thorns mashed onto his head, and nailed to a huge cross with huge spikes going through his hands and feet for my sins and everyone else's sins on this entire earth. I'm not going to push religion in this book, but I'm going to say what contributed greatly to my 'courage to change'. At the end of the movie, when Jesus finally died on the cross, said "It is finished", and gave up his spirit, I actually got, for the first time in my life, what the crucifiction, death, and resurrection of Jesus Christ was all about. And I found that I loved him for it. Shaleen and I were both in tears, snot running out of our noses; just pure heartfelt acceptance for the man that lived a sinless life here on earth and was crucified, died and then raised from the dead three days later by God Himself. It is all documented in the Holy Bible, in the Book of John, for anyone who wants to look it up for verification His arrest starts in chapter 18, his death in John 19 and his resurrection in John 20.

I didn't change overnight, although I believed in Jesus Christ from that day forward. I still had a lot of anger and couldn't trust my fellow human beings; I even had hate but we stayed clean and sober. Shaleen was still staying between her parents' and her brother's, and with me at the sober living house on the weekends. There was just me and another guy living there the whole time and it was a huge 5 bedroom house.

They say in NA to go to 90 meetings in 90 days. I went to 200 meetings in 90 days. I was on fire for recovery. In January of 2006, my doctor released me back to work. My first test in recovery came because my disability benefits were gone which meant I couldn't live at the sober living house. I needed a job! Someone in our recovery group wanted to sell me a huge 5th wheel trailer and said I could make payments. Shaleen's brother, Charles, let us put it at their place.

The logging company gave me my job back now that I was clean and sober. What a break! So, I went back to work, and all the guys were proud of me. They could see the change. That just fed the fuel for my recovery. People that I would run into now and then that knew me before I got clean asked me if I was on the juice, steroids. Ha, ha! Because I was healthy, healthy, healthy! I would just laugh and say no, I'm in recovery. Life seemed great. The kids were with us a lot. I called Justin and Winston every couple of weeks, as it was expensive to call Canada. I sent my ex-wife money as often as I could and never missed the boys' birthdays. I was feeling like a human being for the first time in my life. I even bought a second car for five hundred dollars—a little Toyota Celica.

Isiah 61:10
"My soul shall be joyful in my God; for He has clothed me with the garments of salvation. He has covered me with the robe of righteousness" KJV

Mike getting Fit

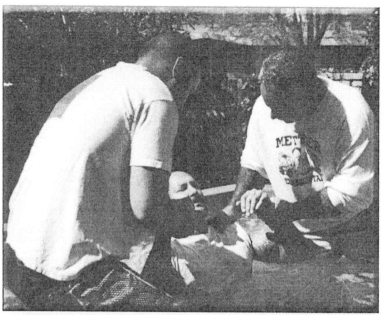

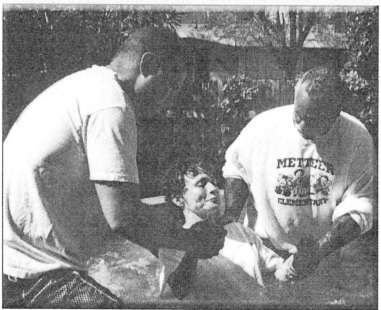

Mike and Shaleeen being Baptized Easter Sunday 2008 by
Pastor Brad Harms and Pastor Mike Hardy

CHAPTER 24
The Toughman Contest

Then one day in May of 2006, I heard a local radio commercial looking for fighters for a Toughman boxing contest at a local casino. That was all me, I thought, so I signed up. The fights were set for June 10th. It was all I could think about. They were only accepting thirty-two fighters, and it went by elimination. You kept fighting if you kept winning. If you lost a fight, you were out. There were 4 weight divisions, so there were eight fighters in each weight division. Each weight division champ would win $1000 and a trophy. I started doing a little training just to brush up a bit since I'd been in lots of fights through the years and in prison. I needed to do some cardio and get my wind up. Fight night came, and for my first fight, the guy they matched me up against didn't look too tough. Let me tell you something, this guy was a bar brawler. In the first round, he knocked me around the ring like a misbehaving stepchild. The fights are all only two rounds. I must admit that I was a little dizzy between rounds. The bell rang for the second round, and this guy came at me, swinging at me like a wild man again. He stepped into my serious straight right punch that I threw with everything I had. It sounded like a baseball bat hitting a pumpkin. Down he went. The ref started the eight count. This guy got up, stumbled around like a bad drunk and went down again. He did this three times, then fell into the ropes. He recovered finally, and we started going at it again. Then the bell rang. The judges gave the fight to him. I was out of it, but it

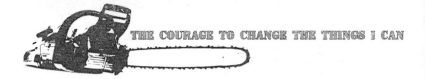

was OK by me because he went on to win the money and trophy, and no one else even came close to beating him, let alone knocking him down.

I saw him the next week at the fair. Both his eyes were about swelled shut, and he told me I punched like a mule kicks. At the fights that night, I met a man by the name of Eli Gonzalez. He's a fight trainer with a gym in Shasta Lake City on the outskirts of Redding. He wanted to train me. They also had fights for women; two heavyweights and two lightweights. Shaleen entered for the fights they were going to have in October. So we started training at Eli's Gym. Eli was inducted into the Martial Arts Hall of Fame in 2006 or 2007, and that's a big deal. His wife, Sarah, and daughter, Rikki, are also a huge part of the gym. They suit up and train every night. They were also inducted into the Martial Arts Hall of Fame in 2008. Such a great family. Everyone that goes there becomes a part of their family.

Psalm 5:12
"For You, O Lord, will bless the righteous; with favor you will surround him as with a shield." NKJV

Eli & Sarah Gonzalez

Shaleen Sparring

Mike in Traning

Mike is on the Program

CHAPTER 25
The Relapse

I got a bomb dropped on me early in July. I got home from work, and the car was gone. As I pulled up, I could sense something was wrong. I checked the fifth wheel trailer and no one was inside. I walked to Charles and Wendy's house, and there I found Shaleen, high as a kite on meth. My heart sank to the floor. As I put up my defenses, all I could say was, "Where is the car?" She could barely even talk, but she let me know that the car was up the road a couple of miles. She had gotten pulled over, and the cops let her walk home, leaving the car there. I don't know how she didn't get arrested. She had no license and was high as ever. The high would also be twice as intense since she was around nine months clean.

As I said, I was heart broken. As I walked two miles to go get the car, I had so many thoughts going through my mind. Mostly, why? We had the same clean date. Shaleen was my best friend and life partner, so, now what? I got the car home, locked it up, and packed enough clothes for work the next day. She was begging me to stay, but I had to make it clear to her that I needed some time to think and that I couldn't be around her in that condition. It isn't safe for people trying to stay clean in recovery to be around people that are using. Shaleen and I had taken each other back out on drugs too many times in the past. The promise I made the day I got clean stood. No matter what, I am not going to get high.

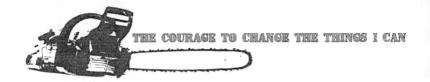

I came home the next night after work and the drugs had worn off. She was so remorseful and felt just terrible. We made up, and things were OK again after a while. I kept my clean date alone. We were training at Eli's Gym three nights a week, getting ready for our fights. It was tough for me because I went to work at 3:00 am. By the time I got home and we drove 40 miles to the gym, did a grueling two hour workout; sparring, heavy bag work, speed bag, more sparring, and then drove home., you could see how I'd be beat. I was in bed at 10 pm and up at 2:30 am. It was tough on me, but that's what real fighters do—no complaints. Plus, I had black eyes every week. What an opportunity to spar with professionals on a regular basis.

Ephesians 3:16
"I pray that out of His glorious riches He may strengthen you with power through His spirit in your inner being." AMP

CHAPTER 26
We're Both Fighting

The fights came, and I ended up fighting this skinny, lanky guy and lost! I was heartbroken! No excuses, looked like ol' Mike Hill had lost it. Shaleen, however, did great. She got second place, but what a fight! Well, I decided I was done after that fight. I still trained a little bit, but getting beat by that guy took the wind out of my sails for quite a while. It all happened in front of a lot of people I know, too. What a lesson in humility. Shaleen went on in the next couple of years to win all three of her fights. I told you she was tough, but she kept relapsing on drugs. I'm not making excuses for her, but she has since been diagnosed with clinical depression. That makes things more understandable.

We also got involved in a little training with an MMA teacher named Avery Vilche. She started her own fight club in Red Bluff, which is still going strong to this day. Besides herself, she has turned out a couple of good fighters. They fight in towns all over the place. However, Shaleen and I were pretty much done fighting by then. Avery is the one who inspired me to write this book. I told her a little bit about my life, and she was always telling me, "You need to write a book about it!" So, I did. When I would get away from it, I would see her, and she'd tell me, "Get in that book, Mike!" So I did.

I finally had to move as the relapses came more and more. I couldn't be around it. Shaleen ended up in another overdose about a year and a half ago, and they locked her up in a mental health facility in Sacramento for a while. She was able to get all

117

her meds up to par, and she has been clean ever since.

Our life together has had many ups and downs; however, our love for one another has always overcome the bad.

I've been living in Red Bluff for four years now, mainly because it's where I got clean. Shaleen comes down a few nights each week to be with me, and I have the kids down. I joined the Laborers Union a number of years back, and it was the best career decision I've ever made. I've been doing bridge construction this whole time.

Proverbs 16:3
"Commit to the Lord, whatever you do, and your plans will succeed." NIV

Shaleen is on the Program

CHAPTER 27
Going To See My Sons

Last November, Shaleen and I, Jayce and Kacey flew down to San Diego for Thanksgiving with my mom. Mom gave me an old VHS tape that was made just shortly after my two sons, Justin and Winston, got to Canada. The pain I felt wasn't a poor me, pitty-pot pain. It was a woulda, coulda, shoulda pain about Mike is changing his life, and he is never going to let that kind of thing happen to him again. After I saw that tape, I felt a tug on my heart so very strong that I started looking into ways and means of getting myself to Canada. First I prayed about it. I talked to my pastor, Dan Woolery. He set me up to talk to a travel agent he knows. That next week at work, I got the main boss to the side and asked if I might be able to take two and a half weeks off in March, which was three months away at the time. I told him I wanted to see my two sons; that I hadn't seen in ten years. He said that would be fine.

So I made all the arrangements three months in advance. I got a round trip airline ticket from Sacramento, California, to Portland, Maine. I covered all my bases and booked a hotel. From Portland, I'd be traveling the rest of the trip, 600 miles, by bus, since no passport was needed to enter Canada by land or sea until June 9th. I had my birth certificate, my ID and my social security card. I let my ex-wife and the boys know I was coming. I told the boys that if, for some reason, I didn't make it across the border, I wanted them to know that I did everything I possibly could to get there.

The next three months went by, and when I got my check

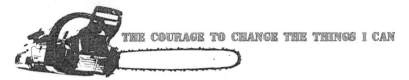

that last day at work, boy, I was so excited! I knew this felt right, and I deserved it. I had done so well getting clean, sending money as often as I could, never missing a birthday or Christmas present. Most importantly though, I had a relationship, even though it was long distance and over the phone--I call every weekend and sometimes during the week--I have an actual relationship with my sons. And I miss them so, so much.

Shaleen and her mom gave me a ride to the airport. I flew all night long and all morning long, not landing in Portland until two p.m. the next day. I got my room and exchanged some currency for Canadian money. I got on a bus the next day for four hours to Bangor, Maine. There, I had to catch a Canadian bus. I paid for round trip tickets with the final destination being where the boys lived. I was so excited and expectant of all going well. What a reunion this would be.

Six hours later, after going through the state of Maine and what seemed like wild lands forever—you could look out the window and see wild turkeys, moose, and deer—we finally got to the Canadian border, to a little town called Calais, Maine. At that point, the two countries are separated by a river a hundred yards wide, . At the bridge which separates the two, there was a U.S. border patrol station and another station on the Canadian side. When the bus pulled around back, out came what looked like a goon squad, straight out of prison. That's what they looked like, a rough, rag tag bunch of prison guards. There isn't anything nice about them, either.

As we pulled up, I zipped my brand new Carhart jacket clear up under my chin to hide my multitude of tatoos. I got my baseball cap screwed on straight and had my documents all in hand and ready. First they sent a dog down the aisle of the bus. That dog went straight for a guy's backpack at the back of the bus and started making all kinds of commotion. They

Going To See My Sons

yanked that guy off the bus so quick, and had him gone, out of sight, like the snap of a finger. Then they split up and worked their way down the aisle hitting everyone up. One of them got to me and I handed him my papers. He asked, "What's your business in Canada? How much money have you got? What do you do for a living? When are you leaving Canada?" I mean, they drill you. He handed me my papers back and said, "Have a nice trip." All I could do was go, Whhheeewww!

Psalm 139:23, 24
"Search me, O God, and know my heart; test me and know my anxious thoughts."
"See if there is any offensive way in me, and lead me in the way everlasting." NIV

A recent photo Wiston and Justin

CHAPTER 28
Inside A Canadian Jail

As the goon squad departed the bus, I really thought I was home free. The bus then crossed the bridge. At the other end of the bridge, we went through the same process, only these officers all had accents, eh? When my series of questions were finished, the officer handed me a yellow slip of paper and told me to depart the bus and go inside the building to the secondary screening and it should only take a minute. Although I had done nothing wrong, I felt like my heart was going to explode through my chest! I got inside and walked up to the counter,.There was an officer there at the computer. He takes the yellow slip of paper from me, and asks, "OK, Mr. Hill, first I must ask, have you ever been arrested? Any tickets, DUI, anything like that?" I said no, of course. He said ok as I heard him rattling the keyboard a million miles an hour. And I thought to myself, 'You've learned in your experiences since getting your life on track that honesty is always the best policy.' So, I piped up and told him that I've had a DUI. You see, I found out that they consider a DUI a felony in Canada. He then said 'ok' and nothing else? And I just couldn't lie, so I told him I'd been arrested more than 100 times and I'd been to prison twice.

I had let loose with this mainly because I saw the bus pulling away and the cops and dogs ripping all my belongings apart. My nice, clean, folded clothes looked like dirty laundry when they were done with it. Next thing I know, I'm thrown into a cell! Wow, my life of the last three years started flashing before my eyes. I couldn't believe it. Not only did what was

supposed to be the happiest moment of my life just disappear with a cloud of diesel smoke and the slam of the jail cell door, but now I've been locked up abroad.

I spent what seemed like hours and hours in there. These guys dragged up everything I'd ever done that was against the law and that I had gotten arrested for since the first time I went to juvenile hall! When they were finally set to let me go, they reviewed all my arrests with me and took a picture of me and made it very clear that I was banned from Canada for life. They let me know that if I ever got caught trying to enter again, I would be subject to ten years in their prison. They packed all my belongings back in my suitcase, and two officers, along with the dog, escorted me back across the bridge and turned me over to the authorities on the U.S. side of the bridge. And, boy, oh, boy, now I got treated like a convict. I had spent the last three years of my life putting all the prison time behind me and here it was raising it's ugly head.

Well, the Americans tousled me up a bit, but within an hour, I found myself free, looking at miles and miles of Maine wilderness. I asked the American Border guard, as he walked me away from the station, "Now what? How am I supposed to get out of here and back to Portland? Hitchhike?" He told me my best bet would be to come back here to the station in two days at precisely 3 p.m. The bus would be coming back through then and that it was up to the bus driver. The nearest motel was five miles away, so I used a pay phone and got a ride to the one and only motel in town. I got in the room and braced myself to make the dreaded phone call to my boys, who were not expecting a phone call, but to see their daddy face to face. I made that heartbreaking call and got it over with. The next day, I found out that this town actually had a

post office, so I mailed Gerri some Canadian money along with a photo album of Justin's first year that she had been wanting. I don't know how I hung on to that through all the years, but it must have been because of sentimental reasons. I also mailed the boys the American Eagle Clothing they had wanted that I had brought as gifts for them.

Two days later at, 2 p.m., I was down at the border station, hoping for a ride on the bus. My odds looked hopeful as the bus pulled up at 2:55 and it was the same driver. After the inspection process, I started walking in the direction of the bus. He waived me over, wheeeww! I was so relieved. He let me on board, and he told me he'd try to get my round trip fare refunded when we got back to Bangor, which he did.

I made it back to Portland and headed straight to the airport. Nope, they told me I'd have to wait a week to get on my regularly scheduled flight unless I wanted to buy a ticket for $650 or more. Naw, I just decided to sit and stew over this for a week, gather myself up and get back home, get back to my job and try to forget this whole mess. I got a motel room, the same one as before. The motel served a continental breakfast in the morning, and I would eat at a buffet place every night. I even joined a gym for the week just to get my mind off of the events that had just taken place. Looking back at it, that whole trip was the most horrible, painful experience I have ever had to go through.

Boy, was I angry with God! But it turns out God does everything for a reason, and although I don't understand what it is yet, I will fully know one day. I do know that I didn't lose my clean time recovery date over it, so that's a real blessing.

A week later, the landing gear tires of flight 1899, chirped down in Sacramento. I was so glad to be back. Shaleen and her brother, Rod, were waiting for me in the lobby. I just didn't know what to feel for quite a while after that. I'm still not completely over that trip as I sit and write this eight months later. But, what happened, happened. I went and talked to Pastor Dan about it. He told me to read the book of Job in the Bible. Let me tell you, that helped me a lot. If you, or someone you know, are really hurting or having some real life difficulties, I strongly suggest reading the book of Job. Any of our problems today are nothing compared to what Job faced, and he stayed faithful to the good Lord through it all and ended up flourishing for staying faithful to God.

Romans 8:35
"Can anything ever separate us from Christ's love?
Does it mean He no longer loves us if we have
trouble or calamity, or are persecuted, or are hungry,
or cold, or in danger or threatened with death?" NLT

Romans 8:37
"No, despite all these things, overwhelming victory is
ours through Christ who loved us." NLT

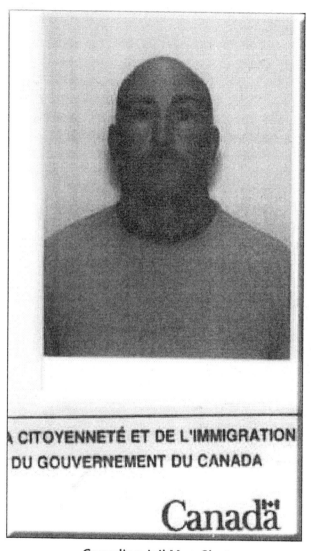

Canadian Jail Mug Shot

CHAPTER 29
The Courage To Change The Things I Can

I went back to work shortly after getting home from that trip, and found the boss had hired a whole gang of guys and laid me off. Talk about bad to worse, huh? I came back from the worst trip of my life, and now I'm unemployed. I argued with him. All he kept saying was, "That's the way it goes." I was stunned, but it all worked out. Although I was totally broke down, I did keep my faith. It was hard to do, but as children of God, we have to realize that *our* ways are not *His* ways. He always has a better plan for us. I was working for another bridge builder the next week. Gotta love the union!

One thing you might be wondering is, with all the dirty needle use and tatoos, did either Shaleen or I come down with anything like HIV or Hepatitis C; both very deadly and very common to drug users. Soon after we got clean, we both got tested for both diseases. We were really scared waiting for the results which seemed to take forever. Thank God we were both free of HIV and Hep C. To be safe, we even had the tests done again a year later. Again, they were both negative. Praise God!

It's all good. Today, we get to be part of peoples' lives, even if a small part. Our niece, Jackie, married a guy named Cliff in September of 2009. We were able to be part of that, as well as being there when she gave birth to baby, Jayden. Today is Oc-

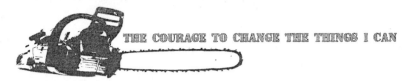

tober 31st, and as I finish this book, I look back through all of my life. I have personally been pulled out of the depths of hell by the loving hands of Jesus Christ. Through Him and His love for me, I am a different person. I just picked up my four years clean coin at N.A. two weeks ago on October 18, 2009. I have loving relationships today with all of my families; adopted and natural born, in-laws, cousins, aunts and uncles. Thanks be not only to God, but to people like Pastor Dan and Laurie Woolery, Pastor Ron and Jerree Largent, Pastor Brad and Susan Harms and family (He is a cop in the San Francisco Bay area), Pastor Mike Hardy and son Woody, I can handle life today, clean and sober and full of the Holy Spirit. I know I will see Justin and Winston one day soon, and what a reunion it will be. (That will be in my next book)

I'm learning about life. All I know today is this; it's full of ups, it's full of downs, but the quality of the life we live all depends on how we act, according to what's dealt to us. Today I feel like I can handle anything that comes to me. I have the courage to change the things I can.

Acts 3:16
"By faith in the name of Jesus, this man whom you see and know was made strong. It is Jesus name and the faith that comes through Him that has given this complete healing, as you can all see." NIV

2 Corintians 5:18-20
All this newness of life is from God, who brought us back to himself through what Christ did. And God has given us the task of reconciling people to him. For God was in Christ, reconciling the world to

The Courage To Change
The Things I Can

himself, no longer counting people's sins against them. This is the wonderful message he has given us to tell others. We are Christ's ambassadors, and God is using us to speak to you. NLT

If you want to become a Christian today, I believe if you say this prayer from your heart, you will be born again.

Dear God, I realize that I am a sinner and I need forgiveness. I believe that Jesus Christ shed his precious blood and died on the cross for my sins, (and the sins of the whole world) was buried and resurrected. I am willing to turn from sin. I now invite Christ to come and dwell in my heart and life as my personal savior. Amen.

If you just said this prayer from the heart, I believe you are now saved. Try to get to know the Bible and in turn, you'll come to know Christ. Talk to God in prayer daily. He will do amazing things in your life. Join a Bible believing church. Tell others about Jesus Christ. Have you ever seen bumper stickers that say "Christians aren't perfect, just forgiven"? That's how it is. Even after we become Christians, we aren't necessarily perfect because there is no way we can be. We just need to strive daily to do the best we can and trust in the Lord to help us in our shortcomings. And He will. Christians still have fun. We don't have to be stiff or bored. Trust in God, have faith in Jesus, and He will take you places you never even imagined.

John 3:16
"For God so loved the world that He gave his only son so that everyone who believes in Him shall not perish, but have everlasting life." NLT

Shaleen's daughter Kacey

Mike and Shaleen's son Jayce

Shaleen's daughter Lacey

Mike's sister Teri, niece Sarah, nephew Jonas

Mike's adopted Dad Robert holding Justin
and his brother John

Most of Mike's adopted family

Mike's Nephew Austin

Mike's birth mother Kathi, Jeff and sister Megan

Mike's adopted Dad Robert
in Mexico

Shaleen's brothers, sisters in law, nieces and nephews.
Mike missed this picture he was in prison.

Mike's adopted mom Deanna, step father
Dan, holding Justin

Mike and Shaleen's granddaughter Montana

Mike's Grandmother Dorothy
and Grandfather Benton Jones

Mike and Pastor Ron Largent

Now that you have read the book, let me tell you about my good friend and brother Mike Chainsaw Hill. As passionate as Mike was about his life on the wild side, he is even more passionate about his life on the God side. There is a reason for that, now he no longer walks in the dark but in the light as an ambassador for the King of Kings.

Mike reminds me of Moses when he came down off Mt. Sinai and his face shone like the sun. When Mike walks into a room, it lights up because that same God who shone through Moses, also shines through him. Mike fell in love with Jesus and seeks Him as if He were buried treasure, and he found what everyone can find, a first love experience that deepens every day. Friends let me tell you that Mike Chainsaw Hill is the real deal. The once famous saying "I want to be like Mike" applies to Mike Hill. However, it is not his glory that draws people to him, it's God's, and the reason is... Mike wants to be like Jesus... do you?

In Christ's love, Pastor Ron Largent

Pastor Dan, with Mike and Shaleen

Mike tells his story his way and it is a good one. For every addict who wonders if there is hope, Mikes offers fresh, honest answers. This is an often painful, but always engaging story of one man's journey from the depths of addiction to freedom in Jesus Christ.

Pastor Dan Woolery

If you don't believe that God can use Chainsaw Mikes testimony, then you have placed God in a box and limited His power.

"When I am with those who are oppressed, I share their oppression so that I might bring them to Christ. Yes, I try to find common ground with everyone so that I might bring them to Christ. I do all this to spread the Good News, and in doing so I enjoy its blessings." I Corinthians 9:22,23 NLT

- Pastor Brad Harms

You can email Mike Hill at chainsaw.mike@hotmail.com or post a comment at www.thecouragebook.blogspot.com. To order books, visit www.accentdigital@gmail.com (530-223-0202)